Going to Live

in New

Zealand

howtobooks

If you want to know how...

Getting a Job Abroad
The international jobseekers' directory

Getting a Job in Australia
A step-by-step guide to finding work in Australia

How to Retire Abroad
Your complete guide to a new life in the sun

Living & Working in Australia
All you need to know for starting a new life 'down under'

Getting into Australia
The complete immigration guide to gaining your visa

howtobooks

Please send for a free copy of the latest catalogue:

How To Books
3 Newtec Place, Magdalen Road,
Oxford OX4 1RE, United Kingdom
email: info@howtobooks.co.uk
http://www.howtobooks.co.uk

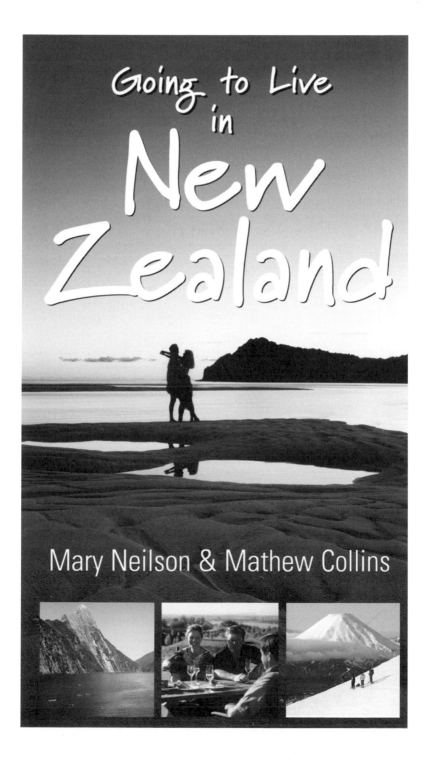

Going to Live in New Zealand

Mary Neilson & Mathew Collins

Published by
How To Books Ltd
3 Newtec Place, Magdalen Road
Oxford OX4 1RE, United Kingdom.
Tel: (01865) 793806. Fax: (01865) 248780.
info@howtobooks.co.uk
www.howtobooks.co.uk

© 2004 Mary Neilson and Mathew Collins
Reprinted 2005

British Library Cataloguing in Publication Data
A catalogue record for this book is available from the British
Library.

Cover design by Baseline Arts Ltd, Oxford
Produced for How To Books by Deer Park Productions,
Tavistock, Devon
Typeset by PDQ Typesetting, Newcastle-under-Lyme, Staffs.
Printed and bound by Cromwell Press, Trowbridge, Wiltshire

NOTE: The material contained in this book is set out in good
faith for general guidance and no liability can be accepted
for loss or expense incurred as a result of relying in particular
circumstances on statements made in the book. The laws and
regulations are complex and liable to change, and readers should
check the current position with the relevant authorities before
making personal arrangements.

Contents

AMBLER COLLINS
IMMIGRATION & COMMERCIAL CONSULTANTS

Dear Reader

Thank you for reading my book.

This probably means that you have some interest in migrating to New Zealand and want to know about starting a new life in a new country.

New Zealand has its own immigration legislation, policies and procedures. These policies are usually reviewed, changed and fine tuned by them on an annual basis.

Your application will have individual circumstances which will be unique to you. Factors taken into consideration can include your qualifications, work experience, training, age, capital resources, family relations and business experience, to name just some. The process can be long and costly and very disappointing if you get it wrong.

So how do you know if you will qualify?

The first step in any migration strategy is to have your personal circumstances assessed against the various categories and criteria to determine your suitability.

My company, AmblerCollins Visa Specialists was established in the early 1990's and is the longest established multi-destinational visa consultancy in the UK. Over the years we have helped many thousands of clients achieve their dream of starting a new life in a new country. If it is possible to get you to your country of choice we will definitely get you there.

As a way of saying thank you please feel free to take up my **FREE ASSESSMENT OFFER**.

Good Luck

Mathew Collins

*To take advantage of our Free Assessment offer please e-mail to: **info@amblercollins.com**
In your email please include "How To Books - Free Assessment Offer" in the subject line or call me or one of my team on **020 7371 0213***

Eden House, 59 Fulham High Street, London SW6 3JJ Telephone: (020) 7371 0213 Fax: (020) 7736 8841
e-mail: info@amblercollins.com   Internet http://www.abmblercollins.com

Introduction

New Zealanders are fiercely independant as a result of their ancestors' resolve to escape a very traditional society. The colonists were determined to hack a new way of life in this very rugged country through hard work and mutual respect for every person, irrespective of birth and status in life. All New Zealanders' ancestors endured long sea journeys to migrate here.

First, Maori arrived in their open wooden sailing craft followed hundreds of years later by those from the United Kingdom in wooden sailing ships. It is a fair comment to say that 'the sea is in every New Zealander's blood'. Of course today most arrive by air.

Asked by a photographer to show his brightest smile as he was leaving New Zealand in 1934, George Bernard Shaw commented, 'If I showed my true feelings I would cry. It's the best country I've been in.' A comment that is reiterated by those who visit today.

NORTH ISLAND

Kaitaia

Whangarei

AUCKLAND
Pokeno

Tauranga

HAMILTON
Rotorua
Opotiki

Gisborne

New Plymouth

Napier

Hawera
Hastings

Wanganui
Palmerston
North

Woodville

Masterton

WELLINGTON

Takaka

Nelson
Blenheim

Westport
Murchison

Inangahua

SOUTH ISLAND

Springs
Jctn.

Kaikoura

Greymouth

Waipara

CHRISTCHURCH

Lake Paringa

Haast

Timaru

Omarama

Oamaru

Milford Sound

Palmerston

Queenstown

Te Anau

Lumsden

DUNEDIN

Invercargill

Milton

N

0   50   100   150 Miles

0   50   100 150 200kms.

New Zealand.

Introducing New Zealand

New Zealand offers a microcosm of all the world's natural environments – active volcanoes, thermal geysers, boiling mud, ancient virgin rainforests and forests of kauri, some of the most awesome trees on earth. There are glaciers descending into rainforests, dolphins to swim with, whale-watching boat trips, or you can fish for trout in clear lakes and streams, walk on remote beaches where there are no other foot prints and enjoy more than 18,000 kilometres of coastline with numerous isolated islands for anchoring your boat.

When cruising spectacular fiords, fur seals and penguins swim and follow the boat. If you are feeling adventurous there is heli-skiing near boiling craters, white-water and cave rafting, rock and mountain climbing, bungee jumping and skydiving. New Zealand is a unique environment with a dramatic landscape, inimitable culture, friendly people, and a myriad of adventure activities.

THE FIRST PEOPLE

When Maori explorers arrived from Polynesia approximately 800–1,000 years ago, (although perhaps Moriori were there first) New Zealand was probably the last place on earth to be peopled. It was certainly the site of the world's most recent violent and destructive volcanic activity. Much of the land today is still untouched by man and some areas may look a little similar to the landscape that greeted those early, fearless and daring sailors who sighted this 'antipodal terra firma'.

The tale of daring Maori sailor, Kupe's discovery of New Zealand, and how his wife, Hine-te-aparangi, named the North Island of Aotearoa, 'Land of the Long White Cloud', is woven into the tukutuku panels found inside some of the meeting houses on different maraes. Legends describe how the rascal Maui, half god, and mythical hero, after a huge struggle fished Te Ilka-a-maui, the Great Fish Maui, the Northern Island of Aotearoa from the sea god, Tangaroa.

This tale is almost an analogy for New Zealand's tortured landscape, which was caused by great volcanic upheavals. The resulting pyrotechnic effects were recorded by Historia Augustus, a Roman document which noted that before 186AD, the sky was 'seen to burst into flame'. Furthermore, at about the same time the Chinese wrote of a sky that was 'as red as blood' for many days. Both examples are interesting evidence that places this youthful land in context with world history and is also a human record of some of the activity that created New Zealand's spectacular 'Middle-earth' terrain.

Maori oral history and the School Journal taught generations of young New Zealanders the tale of how five canoes, Tainui, Aotea, Te Arawa, Tokomaru and Taki-timu, arrived on the shores of New Zealand bearing descendants of each tribe. They brought the vegetable kumera, hunting and fire-making skills to a land where the plethora of vegetation allowed the growth of insects like wetas, giant crickets and also provided the habitat for the prehistoric tuatara (which was extinct in other parts of the world 100 million years ago). There was an abundance of food: shellfish, fish, flightless birds (like the three metre tall moa, kiwi and takahe), birds that flew but are now extinct (the native duck, many songbirds, giant geese and harriers, and the largest eagle on earth), and the edible fern root. Initially, apart from native bats, there were no mammals or predators to disturb the peace of this paradise which was home to many birds that lacked the 'flying gene' and never developed wings, or needed to.

Feathers and wild flax were used to make clothing, and later, as the avian population dwindled, the skins of dogs and rats, initially introduced to supplement food stocks, were also used. As the demise of the birds caused the plentiful food supply to lessen, Maori became more territorial and sought to obtain better land for cropping and to settle on, just as mankind worldwide has done throughout the centuries.

Maori discovered two islands that were quite different in New Zealand. Most welcoming was the warmer climate of the North Island with native forests, the still active and stark volcanic landscapes of Tongariro National Park and

Taranaki, the inviting thermal area of Rotorua and Lake Taupo and many wonderful beaches.

In contrast, the magnificent snow-capped Southern Alps dominated the cooler, very wet and extremely rugged South Island, which, although a difficult area for crop cultivation, provided a perfect habitat for the moa, with a bountiful food supply. Here, Maori named the South Island Te Wai Pounamu after their discovery of valuable repositories of pounamu, the highly prized and more commonly named greenstone (jade or nephrite). Difficult to obtain in treacherous transalpine areas, and equally difficult to carve in what was basically a stone-age culture (there was little in the way of metal other than gold), pounamu ornaments or mere (warclubs) were greatly treasured. The mana, or prestige of these items increased as they were passed on down through generations. Maori carved tiny man-like figures with enlarged heads and symbolic poked out tongues of great mana, which were revered as tokens of fertility. Other shapes represented the coiled fern shape or spiral, hei matau (fishhook) or taniwha (monster) and marakihau (sea monster). Many of these carvings and figures can be seen today in the artistic and intricate traditional designs of waka (war canoes), whare whakiro (meeting houses), sacred feather boxes and other items.

Moko, facial tattoos that made Maori look very fearsome to their own kind and especially those from foreign lands, represented an individual's ancestry. As wars were fought, mainly for land, lost or won, an individual's mana increased by his daring, warlike manner and prowess in battle.

In 1642, Commander Abel Tasman was the first European to sight and name Niuew Zeeland after Zeeland in Holland. He didn't stay long, as three of his crew were murdered when he attempted to land in what he called Murderer's Bay, now known as Golden Bay, near Nelson in the South Island where the golden sand for building construction comes from. Next, between 1769 and 1779, the renowned British explorer Captain James Cook discovered and mapped New Zealand naming many places like Young Nicks Head in Gisborne after the lad who first sighted land. Banks Peninsula, Christchurch, which Cook thought was an island, was named after the esteemed naturalist Sir Joseph Banks.

The French also left their mark as the French explorer Jean-Francois Marie de Surville was sailing around New Zealand about the same time as Captain Cook, but the two never met, even though they were both off the coast of the North Island at about the same time. In 1838, a French whaler, Jean Langlois negotiated the sale of Banks Peninsula with Maori and later returned with 63 settlers. The British reacted promptly and raised their flag at Akaroa claiming sovereignty under The Treaty of Waitangi. Eventually the French did settle at Akaroa, which still retains a French flavour today.

LEARNING TO LIVE TOGETHER

Next, itinerant sealers and whalers arrived – mainly for provisions and respite from their endeavours. Sadly, in an effort to secure a living and to satisfy worldwide growing trades in consumer items like fur, whale meat, oil and bone, the hunter/traders rapidly decimated their seagoing prey. *Moby Dick*, Herman Melville's engrossing tale of whaling, makes reference to the keenly sought after preserved Maori heads, which the whalers traded as souvenirs on their travels. They also introduced prostitution, disease and firearms. Unfortunately Maori, especially Northland's Ngapuhi tribe led by the esteemed warrior Hongi Hika, embraced this new form of weaponry and the subsequent lethal consequences of warfare. The slaughter of the Musket Wars began.

Christianity was introduced by Samuel Marsden in 1814 and the Bible was translated into Maori, the first time that Maori had a written language. During the early 19th century, The New Zealand Immigration Company was formed to provide assisted immigration for residents of the British Isles.

Meanwhile the Maori population continued to decline, as lawlessness between all parties prompted the English to despatch James Busby in 1833 as British Resident in an effort to protect the settlers and maintain law and order. Dubbed 'the man of war without guns' because of his lack of support and authority he was succeeded by Captain William Hobson, who persuaded Maori chiefs to relinquish their sovereignty to the British Crown by signing The Treaty of Waitangi on 6th February 1840. The Queen of England, in return, promised to protect and grant Maori people the rights and privileges of English citizens. Unfortunately the English interpretation of the Treaty was different to Maori understanding. New Zealand's founding document was to become a major source of conflict between different Maori tribes and government representatives culminating with the Land Wars and the confiscation of huge tracts of Maori land by the government and English troops. Unease simmered causing a dissension that continues today.

BREAKING NEW FRONTIERS ON THE SHEEP'S BACK

The export of live sheep in 1834 was the beginning of a major agricultural trade, which developed trading primarily on wool. With the advent of refrigerated ships, the meat, butter and cheese industry thrived. In 1882 the first cargo left the South Island heading for European markets. The discovery of gold in Central Otago, South Island in 1861, just ten years after gold had put Australia on the map, led to a huge migration of Chinese, Australians and Europeans.

New Zealand became a self-governing British colony in 1856 and Maori were given the right to vote in 1867. Wellington became the capital in 1876. Towards the end of the 19th century, 'King Dick' Richard Seddon steered New Zealand through a phase of remarkable and sweeping social change, which included minimum wage structures, old-age pensions, the introduction of arbitration courts and children's health services. This young developing country, formed by pioneers keen to escape the harsh, archaic and often unjust traditions of class, sought to create a nation where all were treated in an equal and fair way by the law of the land. In a world first, suffragette Kate Sheppard lobbied to give women the vote in 1893, 25 years before the British or the Americans.

Although Europeans remained separate from Maori, who tended to retreat to isolated rural areas, intermarriage was common. By the 1900s, when the outlook was bleak, as their population had fallen to approximately 40,000, Maori developed leaders who negotiated to have a political voice and representation in Parliament. The Young Maori Party lobbied for health services and better education.

Many of the great names recognised by New Zealanders today came from this time of renewal. Apirana Ngata of the Ngati Porou tribe became Minister of Native Affairs. James Carroll, Ngati Kahungunu tribe, Maui Pomare, of Tainui and Peter Buck, Ngati Toa all lobbied the Labour party which, on achieving power in 1935, legislated employment equality and increased spending on education, housing and health for Maori.

Although rugby followers everywhere recognised Maori prowess on the field there was still little interaction between both groups of New Zealanders. In the Boer War and the First World War, New Zealand supported the British and participated, incurring heavy casualties of young men, particularly Maori. One in three New Zealand men aged between 20 and 40 years were killed or wounded in the First World War. Each year New Zealanders remember the bravery of these men on Anzac Day (Australia and New Zealand Armed Corps), April 25th.

By 1947, New Zealand was fully independent and enjoying prosperity as the world economy was rebuilt and prices for agricultural products were high. Her social welfare system was the envy of many countries and New Zealanders benefited from one of the world's highest per capita incomes. Growth of the fruit and tobacco industries which required labour encouraged immigration.

When the Korean War (1950–1953) started, Australia, New Zealand and America signed the ANZUS defence pact pledging mutual aid in the event of attack. New Zealand also joined the anti-communist SEATO (South-East Asia Treaty Organisation) and, in 1971, joined the South Pacific Forum, a platform for Pacific governments to discuss common problems.

In the late 1960s there was a revival in Maoritanga (Maori culture) alongside land disputes and increased radicalism, which led to the rise of black power groups. The Race Relations Act, 1975 and the resurrection of the Treaty of Waitangi in 1994 led to the government promising a one billion dollar payout to settle Maori land claims. The Maoritonga renaissance fostered Maori language, literature and art and the establishment of Te Kohanga Reo (language nest for children).

There is still a deep-seated feeling of unease at the dominance of the European culture which occasionally erupts, especially amongst the young (for example the Maori 1995 occupation of Moutoa Gardens in Wanganui). Generally, aided by legislation New Zealanders today have a growing awareness of Maori rights and culture and are proud of the essence that flavours this modern and unique country. The time is right for people of different cultures to respect and live alongside each other in harmony.

New Zealand Today

Radical restructuring since 1984 has moved New Zealand from a government-controlled economy and welfare state to a deregulated and private open market economy that is markedly less of a welfare state. The loss of the traditional European markets for agriculture and the oil crisis in the 1970s caused a fall in the economy which was then exacerbated by the worldwide stock market collapse in 1987. First under a Labour and then a National government, tariffs were lowered, the NZ dollar floated, exchange controls abolished, and overseas borrowing and foreign investment restrictions were reduced. Agriculture subsidies were also removed and a new tax, GST (Goods and Services) was introduced and company and personal income taxes were lowered. In 1983, the CER (Closer Economic Relations) agreement was signed by Australia and New Zealand to allow free and unrestricted trade between the two countries.

In 1984, the Labour Government privatised state industries and Prime Minister David Lange refused entry to all nuclear equipped and powered warships. (To New Zealand's horror, in 1985, French spies bombed the *Rainbow Warrior* in Auckland harbour. The Greenpeace flagship was protesting against nuclear testing at the Moruroa atoll in French Polynesia by the French.)

These economic reforms have dramatically changed New Zealand's focus which, coupled with 'user pays' and cutbacks in social services, means there is now a greater disparity in income levels. Although still reliant on export income from agriculture (mainly beef and veal, dairy products, fish, forest products, fruit and vegetables), diversification into tourism and service industries, manufacturing and small-scale industry means New Zealand has a broader worldwide outlook. Consequently the ideal of an equal society has receded.

In 1995, Sir Peter Blake led the successful challenge for the America's Cup which New Zealand again won against all odds in 2000. In 1999, New Zealanders elected their first female Prime Minister, Helen Clarke, who also led the Labour party to a second victory in 2003.

A DIVERSE CULTURE

New Zealand's population in the 21st century is the result of 150 years of immigration originating mainly from the United Kingdom. In the last 20 years New Zealand has become a very cosmopolitan society embracing a wide diversity of cultures which has resulted in many differences in customs, food, religion and language. Auckland has a strong Polynesian (Pacific Rim countries and Pacific Islands) and East Asian character (Chinese, Japanese,

Korean, Singaporean, Malaysian and Thai.)

Four per cent of the population speak or understand an Asian language. The Indian community is well established and respected throughout both islands. Over the years, Dutch, Finnish and, more recently, Russians and Iranians have made New Zealand their home. With approximately only 14 people per square kilometre, and a total population of nearly four million, the government has implemented immigration incentives to increase this.

Immigration

New Zealand is one of a number of countries in the world that uses immigration policy to contribute towards achieving economic and social objectives.

With a three-year electoral cycle and a political system of proportional representation, New Zealand immigration policy frequently changes. In today's fast moving world with modern telecommunications and computing infrastructures, governments can quickly and accurately measure the outcome of the immigration programmes and the consequent effects on the economy and society.

The purpose of this book is to assist people who are looking for information on the current policy and want to make New Zealand their future home. The book includes advice and information to assist you in evaluating your eligibility under current policies and how to go about working your way through the process.

It gives an overview and explanation of the visa categories most relevant to people looking at the skilled, family, work and business categories. We have not, however, aimed to cover New Zealand's policy on humanitarian cases.

The aim of New Zealand policy is to manage immigration for the national advantage. The department responsible for the implementation and management of the government's immigration scheme is the New Zealand Immigration Service (NZIS).

Their responsibilities include:

♦ facilitating the entry of visitors, students, workers and permanent migrants to New Zealand
♦ providing advice on New Zealand's immigration policies
♦ minimising risks to, and maximising the growth of, New Zealand's economy and society through immigration.

The New Zealand Immigration Service has 30 offices employing around 750 staff. There are 15 offices located overseas (eight in Asia, three in Europe, four in the Pacific) and 15 offices in New Zealand, including the National Office in Wellington.

Without doubt an understanding of current policy and procedures is paramount to an applicant's ability to make a successful application under the policy. This book is designed so you can easily evaluate the criteria under each category we cover.

The following categories are explained and an outline of the criteria required is included:

- Skilled Migration Category
- Business Categories (Investment and Entrepreneur)
- Family Categories
- Work to Residence
- Student Categories
- Returning Residents.

SKILLED MIGRATION CATEGORY

The new Skilled Migration Category (SMC) was introduced in December 2003. It replaced the General Skills Category. It is the most common route for people wanting to gain permanent residency in New Zealand who have no immediate family relatives.

Under this skill stream, the main applicant accrues points based on their formal qualifications, offer of employment, work experience, age and their spouse's qualifications.

With the Skilled Migrant Category there is an increased emphasis on finding employment before taking the first step in the application process, which is lodging an expression of interest. This sounds good in theory but whether it will work in practice is yet to be seen. After many years of working in the industry my experience is that it is still a difficult requirement for intending migrants and employers to match employment needs when they are separated by many thousands of miles..

The Skilled Migrant Category aims to match the skills that migrants bring with the skills New Zealand needs. Specifically they are looking to build New Zealand's capacity. This means they are looking for people with skills that will help build sustainable growth and innovation in New Zealand. They are looking for people who will build New Zealand's connections throughout the world and at the same time enrich the communities in which they live.

Successful applicants will be people who meet the prequisites to qualify as skilled migrants, including those who are already working in skilled employment in New Zealand.

An intending skilled migrant is a person who wants to live and work in New Zealand, and who has the skills to contribute to New Zealand's needs and growth opportunities.

Applying for residence under the Skilled Migrant Category involves you submitting an Expression of Interest before applying for residence. In this Expression of Interest you determine the points you may claim as a skilled migrant.

To be considered under this category you need to be of good health, good character, have a reasonable standard of English and be under 56 years of age. You will also need to meet the threshold of 100 points to register an Expression of Interest.

The points system

The points system is designed to allow Expressions of Interest to be ranked so that the New Zealand Immigration Service can extend invitations to apply for residence to people who have the most to offer New Zealand. Points are available for skilled employment in New Zealand, work experience, qualifications and age. Bonus points are available for employment in areas of identified future growth or absolute skills shortage or within identified clusters. Bonus points are also available for employment outside Auckland and for New Zealand qualifications gained in New Zealand over at least two years.

Expressions of Interest that meet the prerequisites and the minimum points score go into the Expression of Interest Pool, where they are ranked from highest to lowest according to their point scores.

The Expression of Interest process

Step one: Complete an initial self-assessment.
Step two: Submit an Expression of Interest.
Step three: The NZIS rank Expressions of Interest and invite those with the top points to apply for residence.

Expressions of Interest will be entered into a pool. They rank Expressions of Interest in the pool from highest to lowest points claimed. The New Zealand Immigration Service then make regular selections from the pool and, after checking, those with the top points will be invited to lodge an application for residence in New Zealand. It is not a case of first in, first served.

If your Expression of Interest is not selected from the pool the first time, it will remain in the pool for three months. If it is still unsuccessful, you will be told that your Expression of Interest has been withdrawn from the pool. You can lodge another Expression of Interest if you wish.

If the NZIS has not selected any Expressions of Interest over a three-month period, all Expressions of Interest will remain in the pool until they make the next selection.

Step four: The NZIS invite you to apply for residence.
If you have been successful, the NZIS will send you an invitation to apply for residence. After you have been invited to apply you will need to send the requested documents and information to support the claims you made in your Expression of Interest – such as passports, qualifications and relevant certificates.

Step five: The decision.
The NZIS will assess your application for residence against Government residence policy and look at your ability to contribute to New Zealand's social and economic development and to settle successfully. They will also undertake further verification of the information you have supplied in your Expression of Interest.

Depending on your ability to demonstrate your potential to successfully settle in New Zealand.

- ◆ your application may be approved and you will be granted a Residence Visa or Permit

or

◆ you may be granted a Work Visa or Permit, which will enable you to establish yourself in skilled employment in New Zealand and help you gain residence

or

◆ your application may be declined.

Requirements of residence

In some cases, if you are granted residence under the Skilled Migrant Category, you may need to meet a number of requirements. If you have an offer of skilled employment:

◆ You must take up that offer of skilled employment within three months of being granted your first residence permit.

◆ You must remain in that employment – or in other skilled employment for which you would qualify for points or bonus points – for at least three months.

◆ If you have been working in skilled employment for less than three months you must remain in that employment – or in other skilled employment for which you would qualify for points or bonus points – for at least three months.

Fees for Skilled Migrants Category

Fees are charged at different stages of the Skilled Migrant application process. These fees help to cover the cost of processing your application. You need to pay the first fee when you submit your Expression of Interest. If you are invited to apply for residence, you will need to pay a second fee when you submit your application for residence. This fee differs depending on the country from which you are making your application. Then, if your application is approved in principle, you will need to pay a Migrant Levy.

When completing your Expression of Interest, you need to be honest in answering the questions. The NZIS may not accept your Expression of Interest or may decline your application if, at any time, you:

◆ provide false or misleading information
◆ withhold any information that may influence their decision
◆ fail to make them aware of a change in your circumstances that could influence their decision.

If your application is declined for any of the above reasons, you will have no right to appeal their decision.

THE POLICY AND RULES

Age
The NZIS are looking for people who can make a long-term contribution to New Zealand and therefore you must be under 56 years of age to submit an Expression of Interest. People who are 56 and over cannot be approved for residence under the Skilled Migrant Category.

Health
The NZIS need to be assured that you and any family members with you are healthy. They make this require-

ment to safeguard the well-being of New Zealanders and to avoid placing a burden on the country's health and social services.

Your Expression of Interest will not go into the pool if:

* there is any likelihood you will need dialysis treatment
* you have active tuberculosis
* you have required either hospital or residential care for a mental disorder or intellectual disability for more than 90 days in the last two years
* you have a physical incapacity that requires full-time care.

If you are invited to apply for residence you need to have a doctor assess your health and fill in New Zealand Immigration Service medical and chest X-ray certificates for each member of your family coming to New Zealand. In some countries, these certificates can only be completed by doctors nominated by the NZIS. You should check with the relevant office for a list of approved doctors. Pregnant women and children under the age of 12 years are not required to submit X-ray certificates unless a special report is required.

Character
The NZIS need to be assured that you and any family included in your application are of good character. They make this requirement to protect the best interests of New Zealanders.

Your Expression of Interest will not go into the pool if you:

◆ have ever been convicted and sentenced to a prison term of five years or more
◆ have been convicted and sentenced to a prison term for 12 months or more in the past 10 years
◆ have a removal order in force against you
◆ have ever been deported from New Zealand or any other country
◆ are believed to have associated with criminal groups or are in some way a danger to New Zealand.

If you are invited to apply for residence you will have to provide police certificates as evidence of your good character.

Certificates are required from:

◆ your country of citizenship
◆ any country you have been in for 12 months or more in the last 10 years, whether on one or more visits.

English language
Research has shown that English language ability assists the settlement of migrants. The NZIS require people to have a reasonable standard of English to ensure they have the best opportunity to settle successfully into work and life in New Zealand. Their requirements apply differently depending on whether you are the principal applicant – the person completing the form – or a non-principal applicant. Non-principal applicants include the partner and/or

dependent children of the person completing the form.

Requirements for principal applicants

As a principal applicant you must provide:

* A recent International English Language Testing System (IELTS) certificate where you gained an overall band score of 6.5 or over in the IELTS General or Academic Module. The certificate must be less than two years old.

or

* A recognised qualification from a course taught entirely in English. If that qualification was gained in New Zealand you need to show the course completion time was over two years, unless it is a post-graduate qualification. For post-graduate qualifications you need to also hold a recognised under-graduate qualification that would qualify you for at least 50 points.

or

* Evidence that you are in current ongoing skilled employment in New Zealand and have been for at least 12 months.

or

* You can prove to the NZIS through other means that you are a competent user of English.

The factors that will be considered include:

* your current country of residence
* countries you may have lived in before
* how long you were in each country

- whether you speak any languages other than English
- your family's ability to speak English
- whether your family members speak any languages other than English
- your previous or current work and the level of English language skills required
- your qualifications and the level of English language skills they required.

In all cases you may still be required to provide an IELTS certificate to confirm you meet their English language ability requirements.

Requirements for non-principal applicants
As a partner or a dependent child aged 16 and older you must:

- show that you meet the required minimum standard of English

or
- pre-purchase English for Speakers of Other Languages (ESOL) training.

Showing you meet a minimum standard of English:

- A recent IELTS certificate that shows you gained a score of five or over in the IELTS General or Academic Module. The test must be less than two years old.

Or
- As a partner you can score points because you are in skilled employment in New Zealand and have been for at least 12 months.

Or you can prove you have:

♦ completed primary and at least three years' secondary schooling at schools using English

♦ completed at least five years' secondary schooling at schools using English

♦ completed a tertiary course of three years or more at institutions using English

♦ hold a minimum of a 'C' pass in one of the following:
  – General Certificate of Education (GCE) 'A' Levels from Britain or Singapore – subjects must include English Language or Literature, or Use of English
  – Cambridge Certificate of Proficiency in English
  – Hong Kong Advanced Level Examinations (HKALE) – subjects must include Use of English
  – University of Cambridge in collaboration with University of Malaya, General Certificate of English (GCE) 'A' levels. Subjects must include English or General Paper.

Or you hold:

♦ an International Baccalaureate – full Diploma in English Medium

♦ an STPM 920 (Malaysia) – 'A' or 'B' pass in English Literature South African Matriculation Certificate, with a minimum 'D' pass in English (Higher Grade)

♦ a South African Senior Certificate, with a minimum 'D' pass in English (Higher Grade), endorsed with the words 'matriculation exempt'

♦ a New Zealand tertiary entrance qualification gained on completing the seventh form.

Or you hold:

♦ a recognised qualification from a course taught entirely in English.

In all cases the NZIS may still require you to provide an IELTS certificate to confirm you meet their English Language requirements.

If you, as the principal applicant, are claiming points for your partner's skilled employment or recognised qualification, your partner must meet the same minimum requirement as you.

THE POINTS SYSTEM FOR THE SKILLED MIGRATION CATEGORY

The points system is designed so that the NZIS can rank Expressions of Interest and extend Invitations to Apply for residence to people who have the most to offer New Zealand. The greater the number of points you qualify for, the greater your chance of gaining an invitation. You need to qualify for at least 100 points to enter the Expressions of Interest Pool (see Figure 1).

Skilled employment

Skilled employment is work that requires you to use significant specialist, technical or management expertise. You may have gained such expertise through completing a recognised qualification or through work experience. Through skilled employment the New Zealand Immigration Service can link skilled and experienced people with employment opportunities that have been identified as necessary for the growth of the nation.

FACTORS	
Skilled employment:	**Points**
Current skilled employment in New Zealand for 12 months or more	60
Offer of skilled employment in New Zealand or current skilled employment in New Zealand for less than 12 months	50
Bonus points for employment or offer of employment in:	
An identified future growth area, identified cluster, area of absolute skills shortage	5
Region outside Auckland	10
Partner employment or offer of employment	10
Work experience:	
2 years	10
4 years	15
6 years	20
8 years	25
10 years	30
Additional bonus points if work experience in New Zealand:	
2 years	5
4 years	10
6 years or more	15
Additional bonus points for work experience in an identified future growth area, identified cluster or area of absolute skills shortage:	
2 to 5 years	5
6 years or more	10
Qualifications:	
Recognised basic qualification (e.g. trade qualification, diploma, bachelors degree, bachelors degree with honours)	50
Recognised post-graduate qualification (Masters degree, doctorate)	55
Bonus points for:	
Recognised New Zealand qualification (and at least two years study in NZ)	10
Qualification in an identified future growth area, cluster or area of absolute skill shortage	5
Partner qualifications	10
Age (20 to 55 years)	
20–29	30
30–39	25
40–44	20
45–49	10
50–55	5

Figure 1. Skilled Migration Category points table.

Skilled employment	Points
You are currently working in skilled employment in New Zealand and have been for 12 months or more	60
You have an offer of skilled employment in New Zealand or you are currently working in skilled employment in New Zealand and have been for less than 12 months	50

Figure 2. Points available for skilled employment.

To qualify for the points you must show the NZIS that:

◆ your recognised qualification is relevant and that the major subject area directly applies to the employment offered

or

◆ you have expertise that you have gained through relevant work experience in which this expertise was key.

You will only qualify for points:

◆ for genuine full-time employment in which you earn salary or wages or hold a contract position. Positions paid by commission or retainer will not gain points

◆ for ongoing employment

◆ where your employer has a history of good work practices, for example, meeting all New Zealand immigration and employment laws

◆ for employment that meets all New Zealand immigration and employment laws and policies

◆ if your occupation is one that requires occupational registration in New Zealand, you need to prove that you have either full or provisional registration.

Categories of skilled employment

- Major Group 1: Legislators, administrators and managers.
- Major Group 2: Professionals.
- Major Group 3: Technicians and associate professionals, as shown in Figure 3.
- Major Group 7: Trades workers.

Unless the NZIS decide that a special case exists, they do not recognise the following Major Groups of the New Zealand Standard Classification of Occupations as skilled employment:

- Major Group 3: Technicians and associate professionals, except those occupations listed in Figure 3.
- Major Group 4: Clerks.
- Major Group 5: Service and Sales workers.
- Major Group 6: Agriculture and Fishery workers.
- Major Group 8: Plant and machine operators and assemblers.
- Major Group 9: Elementary occupations.

The NZIS may decide a special case exists where:

- your skills would contribute to New Zealand's growth and capacity
  or
- you have, for example, an international reputation and record of excellence in a particular occupation or field.

Work experience

Work experience is the significant specialist, technical or

31111 Physical Science Technician	31121 Quantity Surveyor
31122 Quantity Surveyor's Technician	31123 Clerk of Works
31124 Other Civil Engineering Technician	31131 Electrical Engineering Technician
31141 Telecommunications Technician	31142 Computer Systems Technicians
31143 Other Electronics Engineering Technician	31144 Avionics Technician
31151 Mechanical Engineering Technician	31161 Chemical Engineering Technician
31191 Other Engineering Technician	31192 Non Destructive Testing Technician
31211 Computer Programmer	31213 Computer Support Technician
31331 Medical Radiation Technologist	31332 Other Medical Equipment Controller
31333 Sonographer	31411 Ships' Engineer
31421 Ships' Officer (Deck) including Master	31422 Launch Master
31423 Other Ships' Deck Officer and Pilot	31431 Aircraft Pilot and Flight Crew
31434 Helicopter Pilot	31441 Air Traffic Controller
31511 Safety Inspector	31512 Meat Inspector
31513 Noxious Weeds/Pest Inspector	31514 Health Inspector
31515 Agricultural Inspector	31516 Quality Inspector
32111 Life Science Technician	32112 Medical Laboratory Technician
32121 Agricultural Technician	32122 Forest Technician
32211 Dispensing Optician	32221 Dental Therapist
32231 Physiotherapist	32232 Occupational Therapist
32233 Osteopath	32236 Chiropractor
32234 Orthotist/Prosthetist	32235 Podiatrist
33171 Valuer	33411 Social Worker
33413 Case Worker	33412 Probation Worker
33421 Employment Programme Teaching Associate Professional	33612 Reporter
33613 Editor	33614 Sub-Editor
33631 Graphic Designer	33632 Fashion Designer
33634 Interior Designer	33644 Singing and Music Teacher
33652 Dancing Teacher and/or Choreographer	33662 Artistic Director
33811 Acclimatisation Field Officer	33812 National Park Ranger

Figure 3. Technicians and associate professional categories.

management expertise you have gained through working in your occupation. NZIS awards points for work experience that has given you transferable skills that will help you settle in and contribute to New Zealand.

Years of work experience	Points
2	10
4	15
6	20
8	25
10	30

Figure 4. Points avaiable for work experience.

You may qualify for points if your work experience:

◆ is relevant to your recognised qualification
◆ is relevant to your current or offered skilled employment
◆ is skilled because it required, or enabled you to gain, significant specialist, technical or management expertise.

If you are not currently working in, or have an offer of, skilled employment in New Zealand, your work experience can only qualify for points if it was gained in a comparable labour market. The NZIS recognise the following countries as having a comparable labour market to New Zealand:

Australia	Malaysia
Austria	New Zealand
Belgium-Luxembourg	Netherlands
Canada	Norway
Cyprus	Philippines
Denmark	Portugal
Finland	Republic of South Korea
France	Singapore
Germany	South Africa
Greece	Spain
Iceland	Sweden
Ireland	Switzerland
Israel	United Kingdom
Italy	United States
Japan	

If your work experience was gained in a country that is not listed, that experience will only be assessed as being in a comparable labour market if you:

◆ were lawfully working for a multi-national commercial entity domiciled in one of the listed countries, and
◆ are a permanent resident or citizen of one of the listed countries.

Calculating work experience

Work experience is calculated on complete, full-time weeks of 30 hours. This applies even if you worked more than 30 hours per week. For example, fifty two 60 hour weeks will count as one year's work experience.

If you worked part time – less than 30 hours per week – NZIS will award points according to the hours equating to full-time work. For example, four years of working a 15-hour week will count as two years' full-time work experience.

To be invited to apply for residence under the Skilled Migrant Category, you must qualify for points for either work experience or recognised qualifications.

Recognised qualifications

You can qualify for points for qualifications such as trade certificates, and diplomas, bachelor degrees and post-graduate qualifications. The NZIS provide points for these qualifications as they indicate your ability to gain skilled employment in New Zealand and because qualified people enrich New Zealand's work environment.

Type of qualification	Points
Recognised basic qualification (e.g. trade qualification, diploma, bachelors degree, bachelors degree with honours)	50
Recognised post-graduate qualification (Masters degree, doctorate)	55

Figure 5. Points available for qualifications.

To qualify for points your qualification must be at Levels 4–10 on the New Zealand Register of Quality Assured Qualifications:

Level	Description	Points
10	Doctorates	55
9	Masters degrees	55
8	Postgraduate diplomas and certificates, bachelors degrees with honours	50
7	Bachelors degrees, graduate diplomas	50
6	Graduate certificates	50
5	Diplomas	50
4	Certificates (acceptable trades only – no points will be confirmed for other qualifications at this level)	50
3	Certificates	0
2	Certificates	0
1	Certificates	0

Figure 6. Register of Quality Assured Qualifications – points table.

The level your qualification occupies is determined by:

◆ its alignment to a qualification on the List of Recognised Qualifications
   or
◆ an assessment by the New Zealand Qualifications Authority (NZQA).

If you are invited to apply for residence you will have to provide evidence of the qualification you are claiming points for as well as:

◆ an NZQA Interim Assessment Report – an initial assessment of the level of your qualification based on information supplied by you
   or

◆ an NZQA Qualifications Assessment Report – a full independent assessment and verification.

To be invited to apply for residence under the Skilled Migrant Category, you must qualify for points for either recognised qualifications or work experience.

Age

The NZIS is looking for people who can make a long-term contribution. That is why more points are provided for younger people.

Age	Points
20–29	30
30–39	25
40–44	20
45–49	10
50–55	3

Figure 7. Points available for age.

The NZIS need to see your:

◆ birth certificate
◆ passport or other travel documents
◆ identity card – if you are from a country that requires such cards that confirm your date of birth.

You may qualify for further points:

◆ bonus points for skilled employment
◆ bonus points for work experience
◆ bonus points for qualifications

◆ bonus points for skilled employment.

You may qualify for bonus points if you have an offer of, or are already working in, skilled employment in areas that will best contribute to New Zealand's economic growth.

Bonus points for employment or offer of employment in:	Points
An identified future growth area, identified cluster, area of absolute skills shortage	5
Region outside Auckland	10

Figure 8. Employment bonus points.

Identified future growth area

Currently New Zealand recognises three broad areas of industry that offer considerable opportunity to increase its prosperity.

◆ Biotechnology.
◆ Information communications technology.
◆ Creative industries:
  – advertising
  – software and computing services
  – publishing
  – TV and radio
  – film and video
  – architecture
  – design
  – designer fashion
  – music and the performing arts
  – visual arts.

Your current or proposed employer will need to confirm that they operate in one of these areas.

Clusters

A cluster is a group of employers within a particular industry who, though they may compete with each other, also work together co-operatively to gain greater business advantage. There are currently five recognised clusters – you can gain points only if one of these five is your employer:

1. Film Auckland – a group of entities involved in the Auckland screen production industry, promoting the area as a place to film and arrange production.

2. Wellington Creative Manufacturing – an association of entities involved in creative/niche design and manufacturing in the Wellington region.

3. Canterbury Software – an association of software producers and support agencies who work together to help innovative software companies commercialise their products.

4. Biosouth – a network of biotechnology and related entities whose aim is to generate more wealth from biotechnology for the Otago region of New Zealand.

5. Canterbury Nutraceuticals – a group of entities involved in producing natural, bioactive extracts used in health-promoting and disease-preventing natural products.

Your current or proposed employer will need to confirm they are in one of these clusters.

Area of absolute skills shortage

These areas are occupations that are listed on the Priority Occupations List. You will need to prove that your current employment or offer of employment meets the specifications of the List and that you are suitably qualified and/or experienced for the occupation.

Employment outside Auckland

You may qualify for points if your employment is outside the Auckland region. The NZIS provide these bonus points as they want to ensure all New Zealanders benefit from the skills of immigrants. Your employment will need to be outside these local government areas:

+ Rodney District Council
+ North Shore City Council
+ Waitakere City Council
+ Auckland City Council
+ Manukau City Council
+ Papakura District Council.

You will need to provide proof that your place of work is outside of Auckland.

Partner's skilled employment

You may qualify for bonus points if your partner currently works in, or has an offer of, skilled employment. You must have been in a genuine and stable relationship with your partner for 12 months or more and you must have included your partner in your application. Your partner also needs to meet the same English language requirements as you, the principal applicant.

Bonus points for work experience

The NZIS provide bonus points to people with work experience in New Zealand and in specific areas they determine as being of greatest benefit to New Zealand.

Work experience in New Zealand

The NZIS award you additional points if your work experience was gained in New Zealand. This is because you will have a better understanding of the New Zealand labour market and will find it easier to gain skilled employment and settle.

Additional bonus points for work experience in New Zealand:	Points
2 years	5
4 years	10
6 years or more	15

Additional bonus points for work experience in an identified future growth area, cluster or area of absolute skills shortage:	Points
2 to 5 years	5
6 years or more	10

Figure 9. Additional bonus points for work experience.

Work experience in an identified future growth area or cluster

You may qualify for additional points for work experience in these areas as the NZIS wish to attract people with skills that will benefit New Zealand's economic growth.

To qualify for points, you need to be working in, or have an offer of skilled employment and be able to show that the work experience you have is relevant to that employment.

Work experience in an area of absolute skills shortage

You may qualify for additional points for work experience in these areas as the NZIS wish to attract people with skills that again contribute to New Zealand's growth. To qualify for points, you need to show that your experience is in an occupation on the Priority Occupations List.

Bonus points for qualifications

The NZIS award bonus points to people with recognised qualifications in areas in which skills are in demand in New Zealand.

Bonus points for:	Points
Recognised New Zealand qualification (and at least two years study in New Zealand)	10
Qualification in an identified future growth area, cluster or area of absolute skills shortage	5
Spouse/partner qualifications	10

Figure 10. Qualifications bonus points.

New Zealand qualifications

A recognised qualification gained in New Zealand provides you with a qualification that is relevant to New Zealand employers. This is likely to help you settle in and contribute to New Zealand. NZIS provides points for qualifications that you have studied for and gained through a New Zealand institution such as a university or polytechnic. The qualification requires at least two years' study in New Zealand and must be in an identified growth area or cluster.

You may qualify for points for qualifications in these areas as your skills will help build New Zealand's short- and long-term economic well-being.

To qualify for points you'll need to be working in, or have an offer of, skilled employment in an identified future growth area. To be assessed as relevant, the major subject area of your qualification must directly apply to the skilled employment and that employment must require such a qualification.

If the NZIS select your Expression of Interest from the Expressions of Interest Pool and invite you to apply for residence, they will assess you to see how well you are likely to settle in and contribute to New Zealand. They are looking for people who can offer the most to New Zealand.

Assessing your ability

If you have qualified for points for particular factors you will be assessed as having the ability to settle and contribute. If NZIS make this assessment your application will be approved in principle. You will need to have:

- an offer of, or to already be working in, ongoing skilled employment in New Zealand
  or
- undertaken full-time study for at least two years in New Zealand and as a result have earned:
  - a doctorate or Masters degree, or
  - a qualification in the areas of identified future growth or absolute skills shortage.

The points structure for the Investor Category is shown in Figure 11.

Age	Points	Business experience (years)	Points	Investment funds (NZ$)	Points
25–29	10	2	1	1,000,000	1
30–34	9	4	2	1,500,000	2
35–39	8	6	3	2,000,000	3
40-44	6	8	4	2,500,000	4
45–49	4	10	5	3,000,000	5
50–54	2			3,500,000	6
55–64	0			4,000,000	7
65–74	−2			4,500,000	8
75–84	−4			5,000,000	9
				5,500,000	10
				6,000,000	11

Figure 11. Investor Category points structure.

Business experience

You will be required to provide the following evidence as proof of your ability to claim points within the Investor Category:

- proof of ownership
- business registration
- company accounts or tax returns
- shareholders certificate
- a description of your responsibilities/duties, or a letter from your accountant which covers these points.

Investment funds

With regards to investment funds, you must be able to show that these funds have been earned legally. All documents showing current value must be no more than three months old at the time of application. Acceptable evidence includes:

Cash
- original bank statements
- letters of credit

Property
- original title deeds
- recent valuation from an independent agent
- mortgage document or statements showing any liability incurred on the property
- evidence of the purchase price of the property you provide the valuation for

Shares/Bonds
- a recent statement by a registered broker or accountant certifying the current market value of your shares

Business
- documents of ownership, or financial interest in the company/business, or
- an independent valuation carried out by a chartered accountant, including details of any mortgages, loan(s) or other financial obligations

Other assets
- original ownership certificates
- valuation from independent agent.

In addition, you and any family included in your application must meet health, character, and English language requirements.

ENTREPRENEUR CATEGORY

The New Zealand Immigration Service Business Migration Branch assesses all applications lodged under the Entrepreneur Category. To qualify under the Entrepreneur Category, you must have successfully established a business in New Zealand for a period of at least two years. The business that you have established must benefit New Zealand in some way. In addition, you and any family included in your application must meet health, character, and English language requirements.

You are considered to have successfully established a business in New Zealand if you:

◆ have established or purchased, or made a substantial investment in a business operating in New Zealand; and

◆ have been self-employed in New Zealand in that business for at least two years.

A substantial investment in a business is defined as ownership of at least 25% of a business.

You are considered to be self-employed if you have:

◆ a lawful active involvement in the management and operating of a business in New Zealand which you have established or purchased, or in which you have made a substantial investment.

Your business may be deemed as benefiting New Zealand if it promotes New Zealand's economic growth through:

◆ introduction of new technology, management or technical skills; **or**
◆ introduction of new products or services; **or**
◆ development of new export markets or increased market access; **or**
◆ creation of new job opportunities; **or**
◆ revitalisation of an existing business.

LONG-TERM BUSINESS VISA
The New Zealand Immigration Service Business Migration Branch assesses all applications lodged under the Long-Term Business Visa/Permit category. The Long Term Business Visa/Permit is a special category of work visa/permit and is not a residence category. You may apply under this category if you are a potential migrant interested in applying for residence under the Entrepreneur Category. You may also apply under this category if you are interested in establishing a business in New Zealand but do not wish to live permanently in New Zealand.

To apply under the Long Term Business Visa/Permit category, you must:

◆ have a satisfactory business plan; and
◆ have, in addition to investment capital, sufficient funds for your maintenance and accommodation and that of any non-principal applicants; and

- satisfy the business immigration specialist that you are genuinely interested in establishing a business in New Zealand
- meet English language requirements.

In addition, you and any family members included in your application must meet health and character requirements.

A business plan is a proposal to establish a specific business in New Zealand. This plan must include the following information, and be supported by appropriate documentation:

- an outline of your proposed business and its viability; and
- financial information (forecasts and financing options); and
- your business experience (including English language ability); and
- your knowledge of the New Zealand market.

The business plan is your proposal to establish a business in New Zealand. A business that is started on the basis of sound planning and appropriate professional advice is far more likely to succeed than one started without careful thought and planning.

You are required to complete the business plan detailed in the relevant application form. Your business plan should be no more than three months old at the time you submit your application.

Assessment of business plans

The New Zealand Immigration Service will assess your business plan on the credibility of the information you provide and the knowledge that you display of the proposed business and the New Zealand business environment. Your business plan must be supported by suitable evidence that reflects your research into your proposed venture. Each section of the business plan is assessed separately, but the information you provide in each section should link together and be consistent.

The NZIS will assess your business plan and whether you have:

- **sufficient funds** – enough money to establish your proposed business in New Zealand; and
- **realistic financial forecasts** – your business plan contains realistic financial forecasts; and
- **relevant business experience** – evidence that you have relevant business experience; and
- **sound business record** – you have not been involved in business failure or bankruptcy within the last five years; and
- **sound business character** – you have never been involved in business fraud or financial impropriety; and
- **registration** – you have obtained professional or occupational registration in New Zealand if this is required for your proposed business.

You are required to provide the following information:

Business type

The industry in which your proposed business is positioned.

Location of the business

The location of your proposed business.

Maintenance funds

You must provide evidence that you have, in addition to investment capital, sufficient funds for your maintenance and accommodation and that of any spouse or partner and/or dependent children who are included in your application.

Business status

Whether you intend to establish a new business or purchase an existing business.

Investment capital

Advise and substantiate the amount of funds in NZ$ that you have available to establish or purchase your business and to use as working capital.

Business outline

You are required to supply a business outline, which should include details of the following:

◆ a summary of the business;
◆ the proposed marketing strategy; and
◆ the timeline for establishing the business.

You will need to illustrate your knowledge of your proposed business and how you intend to structure and operate it. You should include:

- a description of the proposed business
- the industry that the business will operate in
- the proposed customers of the business
- where the business will source suppliers
- the intended distribution network of the company
- what assets the company will require.

Expectations
You will need to describe in detail what you expect the business to achieve within its first three years of operation. For example, establishing relationships with suppliers, gaining new customers, employing full-time staff.

Proposed ownership structure
Select the legal structure that is most appropriate to your proposed business. Provide details of the proposed ownership structure of the business including the names of any potential business partners. You are required to have a minimum shareholding of 25% in the business.

Overseas links
Provide details of any relationships that your proposed business will have with any overseas companies. A relationship may include:

- shared ownership
- joint shareholders or directors
- supply agreements
- agency agreements.

Benefit to New Zealand

Detail how your business will promote New Zealand's economic growth. Discuss whether your business will:

◆ introduce, or enhance existing, technology, management or technical skills; or
◆ introduce, or enhance existing, products or services; or
◆ create, or expand existing, export markets; or
◆ create employment (other than for yourself); or
◆ revitalise an existing New Zealand business.

Your role

Describe what level of involvement you intend to have in the proposed business by providing an accurate and detailed job description. Use of a title such as 'Director' without an accompanying job description is unacceptable.

Number of employees

How many full-time employees will your business require within the first 1–2 years of operation? You must advise whether you, your spouse and/or your family are included in this number. In addition, state when you intend to employ these people.

Employees' skills

Provide details of the skills that your potential employees will require. Are these skills readily available in New Zealand?

Marketing strategy

Provide details of how you intend to market your business. These should include:

- the estimated market size in New Zealand
- the business's targeted market share
- how this market share will be achieved
- analysis on the degree of competition in the market
- the business's distribution policy
- any pre-arranged agreements that either the business or you have with suppliers or distributors.

SWOT analysis

Complete a brief SWOT analysis. This should identify the main Strengths, Weaknesses, Opportunities and Threats that will impact on the business. It is to your advantage to explain how any threats or weakness you have identified will be overcome.

Proposed timeline

Provide details of the proposed timeline for establishing the business in New Zealand. You should include in your timeline an estimation of the time required to complete the following:

- establishing the business
- obtaining approvals
- finding premises
- purchasing equipment
- recruiting staff
- establishing a distribution network
- starting operations.

Financial information

You will also need to provide detailed forecast information on the financial performance and position of the proposed business. This includes completing three-year forecast profit and loss statements and cash flow forecasts. You are expected to show an understanding of the revenue and cost structures relevant to the proposed business. You are required to provide detail on how you intend to finance the establishment of the business.

Start-up costs
You will have to provide details of the following expenses:

◆ legal and professional fees
◆ research and development
◆ staff recruitment costs
◆ resource approval costs (Resource Management Act)
◆ business fit-out costs
◆ assets that need to be purchased.

Where an existing business is being purchased or an existing business is operating prior to visa approval, you should include:

◆ any conditional sale and purchase agreement
◆ the basis for the purchase price, i.e. an independent valuation
◆ the profit and loss statement for at least the previous two years as well as actual results to the date of your application. You should comment on the business's past performance and trends.

Profit and loss forecasts
You will need to provide a forecast profit and loss statement. The NZIS advise what ratios must be calculated using the following formulas:

- gross profit margin (%) = gross profit/revenue × 100
- net profit margin (%) = net profit after tax/revenue × 100
- interest cover (times) = earnings before interest and tax/interest expense.

All supporting assumptions should be included. Assumptions should be consistent and link together with other sections of the business plan. The following assumptions are particularly important:

- **Revenue/sales** – explain the basis for forecasts, such as past experience, undertakings from prospective customers, or market research. Where appropriate, assumptions should include number of units and price.
- **Gross profit margin** – as per revenue/sales, the basis for the gross profit margin should be explained and supported. Provide evidence where appropriate.
- **Salaries** – this should reconcile with the number of employees you stated you were intending to employ earlier in your business plan. You must include the cost of full-time and part-time employees.
- **Rent** – as above, explain the basis for your forecast (for example, the cost of the existing lease, the current market rental for equivalent premises).

Although you do not need to include a balance sheet, it is worthwhile including one to show clearly the capital structure and the assets that will be used by the business. It will also be helpful in preparing the cash flow forecast.

Cash flow forecast

A template is provided within the relevant application form for completing the cash flow forecast. You are required to complete all sections and should pay close attention to the section detailing movements in working capital as this will help you to assess cash requirements, this is essential if you are forecasting rapid growth for your business.

You will probably find it beneficial to expand at least the first year to a monthly forecast.

Capital investment required

State the total capital that is required to establish the business. You should include details of any finance that you require to fund initial start-up costs. It would be beneficial to include a table which summarises the funds available and, where applicable, show the net funds available in local currency, the current conversion rate applied, and the resultant funds available in NZ$. This table must be supported by third party evidence such as bank statements. If your funds are invested in property or other assets, you should explain how you are going to utilise them.

Your investment capital

What bank or other finance do you have available to invest in the company?

Additional financing

Will additional financing be required?

Financing arrangements

You must provide evidence that any collateral or guarantors you have available are able to support any funding applications.

Business experience

You are required to provide details of your past business experience, this should include the following:

* how you started in business
* the types of businesses you have been involved with in the past
* detail of specific roles and responsibilities within these businesses
* references from associates, clients, and employers.

Letters of reference must include the physical address, telephone and fax numbers of past employers and businesses. If applicable, these addresses should be provided in both English and your own language.

Your existing business(es)

You need to provide detail on any existing business ventures, including:

* the type of business
* the background of the business
* turnover and profitability
* the number of employees.

You are required to provide documentation in support of your claims, including:

- business registration licences
- financial statements (audited if available)
- copies of tax returns
- contact details for the business
- organisational charts.

Alternatively, you may provide a report covering these points from an internationally recognised accounting firm.

Your shareholdings
Provide details of current shareholdings in any existing business.

Business failures
Provide details of the circumstances surrounding any previous business failure or bankruptcy.

Fraud
Your business plan will not be approved if you have any previous convictions for fraud or financial impropriety.

Qualifications
Provide certified copies of all qualifications.

Registration
Provide evidence that you have obtained professional or trade registration, if this is required in order to operate the proposed business in New Zealand.

Knowledge of the New Zealand market
You are required to illustrate your knowledge of the New Zealand business environment and the impact that this environment will have on your business proposal. It is

essential that you provide evidence that you have conducted sufficient research of the New Zealand market and the factors relevant to your proposed business to enable that business to operate successfully.

Please note that you should demonstrate **your** knowledge, as opposed to that of any other person who may be assisting you to complete your application.

Knowledge of the New Zealand business environment

You should provide details of any knowledge you have of the New Zealand business environment, including any previous dealings or connections with New Zealand businesses. It is essential that the knowledge you convey is specific to the area in which you wish to operate your business. You should provide details of how the current business environment in New Zealand will impact on your proposed business.

New Zealand business involvement

Provide details of any current or previous involvement you have had in terms of owning or supplying a New Zealand business.

Trade associations

If you have been in contact with any relevant trade associations within New Zealand, you should provide evidence of this.

Business research

You are required to provide details of research conducted on the viability of your proposed business. You should include a summary of your research.

Professional advice

If you have received any professional advice with regards to the establishment of a business in New Zealand, you should provide details and supporting documentation.

Resource management consents

Will your proposed business require consents under the Resource Management Act or the Overseas Investment Act? State whether other consents or regulations (for example, health and safety requirements) apply to your proposed business.

Family/associates' business experience

Provide details of the involvement of any of your associates or family members with any similar businesses in New Zealand.

Validity of work visas and permits

If your application is approved you will be granted and/or issued a nine-month work permit and/or work visa to allow you to establish and commence the operation of your proposed business in New Zealand. Further permits and/or visas may be granted or issued for the balance of the three-year period (i.e. 27 months) if:

♦ you apply within the validity of your work permit and/ or work visa; and

♦ you provide satisfactory evidence to demonstrate that your investment capital was transferred to New Zealand through the banking system; and

♦ you provide satisfactory evidence to demonstrate that you have taken reasonable steps to establish or invest in your proposed business.

The requirement for a further application fee at this time will be waived unless a business immigration specialist considers that substantial additional work is required to process the application.

If for any reason you are unable to provide satisfactory evidence of having taken reasonable steps to establish or invest in your proposed business, but it appears that you may be able to provide such evidence within a specified time, a further short-term permit and/or visa may be granted or issued to you to allow you to take further steps to establish and operate your proposed business.

Changing a business proposal

If you wish to change your business proposal within the validity of your visa and/or permit you must seek the consent of a business immigration specialist to the change. Consent may be given if a business immigration specialist is satisfied that:

- you have genuine reasons for abandoning your original business proposal; and
- you have an acceptable business plan for the proposed new business; and
- your new business proposal requires the same or a greater level of capital investment than your original business proposal; and
- you have access to sufficient capital to finance the proposed new business; and
- you have business experience relevant to the proposed new business.

Your permit may be revoked if you undertake a different business proposal to your original proposal without seeking consent from a business immigration specialist.

Note: It is understood that given the fluid nature of business, a business proposal may undergo some modification or further development once put into action. If you are unsure whether a change you are making to your business proposal will require consent from a business immigration specialist, you should contact the business immigration specialist who has been assigned to your case.

Renewal of work permits and visas

Further work permits and/or work visas may be granted or issued to you beyond the initial three-year period (for periods not exceeding three years) if you can satisfy a business immigration specialist that you have valid reasons for needing a further permit.

If you are seeking a renewal for a period beyond the initial three years on the basis of a new business proposal, a business immigration specialist may require that a new application be lodged.

Further work permits and/or visas will be granted or issued only where a business immigration specialist is satisfied that:

◆ any time you have spent in New Zealand has been spent setting up and operating your original business proposal; or

- if you made a change to your original business proposal, consent was granted for that change by a business immigration specialist; and
- you and any family member accompanying you have not drawn on the New Zealand welfare system; and
- you intend to spend the further period in New Zealand either implementing the original business proposed or a subsequent business proposal for which a business immigration specialist has given consent; and
- you have, in addition to investment capital, access to sufficient funds for your own maintenance and accommodation and that of any spouse, partner or dependent children accompanying you; and
- you meet health and character requirements.

Evaluation requirement
In addition to the aforementioned, in the event that your application is approved, you must agree to participate in an evaluation of the Long-Term Business Visa/Permit category for a period of up to five years from the date your application is approved. You must also agree to inform the NZIS of any changes to your postal/contact address within five years from the date of approval of your application for the purpose of participating in this evaluation.

EMPLOYEES OF RELOCATING BUSINESSES
The New Zealand Immigration Service Business Migration Branch assesses all applications lodged under the Employees of Relocating Businesses Category.

If you are an employee of a relocating business and do not qualify under any other residence categories, you may be granted residence under the Employees of Relocating Businesses category on a case-by-case basis. To qualify for consideration under this category, you must be a key employee of the relocating business. In addition, you and any family included in your application must meet health, character, and English language requirements.

A relocating business is a business that proposes to operate in New Zealand.

A key employee is an employee of the business whom the chief executive officer (CEO) of the relocating business reasonably considers will be essential to the operation of the relocated business in New Zealand.

FAMILY CATEGORIES

Partnership
You may be granted residence in New Zealand if you:

◆ are living together (and have been for a minimum of 12 months) in a genuine and stable relationship with a New Zealand citizen or resident; and
◆ meet the minimum requirements under partnership policy, i.e. that you and your partner:
  – are both 18 years or older (or evidence of parental/ guardian/other consent if aged between 16 years and 19 years); and
  – have met prior to your application being made, and
  – are not close relatives.
◆ and meet all other relevant policy criteria.

A partnership may be a legal marriage or an interdependent partnership akin to a marriage (whether heterosexual or same sex).

Note: Holders of valid Australian passports who do not hold current New Zealand residence permits or current New Zealand returning residents' visas; or Holders of New Zealand residence permits or New Zealand returning residents' visas granted on the basis of the person being the holder of an Australian resident return visa, must satisfy an immigration officer that New Zealand is their primary place of established residence at the time their partner's application is made and assessed.

Applicants under partnership policy must be sponsored by their New Zealand partner. A New Zealand citizen or resident is not eligible to sponsor if he or she:

◆ has previously supported or sponsored more than one other successful applicant under partnership policy and that relationship ended as a result of divorce or separation; or
◆ has supported or sponsored any other successful applicant under partnership policy in the last five years and that marriage or relationship ended as a result of divorce or separation; or
◆ was the perpetrator of an incident of domestic violence that has resulted in the granting of a residence permit to a person under the special policy for victims of domestic violence; or
◆ has previously supported or sponsored more than one other successful principal applicant under partnership

policy; or

◆ has previously supported or sponsored any other successful principal applicant under partnership policy in the five years immediately preceding the date the current application is made; or

◆ was a successful principal applicant under partnership policy:
  – if less than five years has elapsed since the date they were granted residence under partnership policy; or
  – if they have previously supported or sponsored any other successful principal applicant under partnership policy.

Note: A person is considered to be the perpetrator of an incident of domestic violence if they have been convicted in New Zealand of an offence of domestic violence against such a person or they were the subject of a complaint of domestic violence against such a person investigated by the New Zealand Police where the New Zealand Police are satisfied that such domestic violence has occurred.

Parent Family Category

You may qualify under the Family Parent Category if you are sponsored by an adult child 17 years or over, who is a New Zealand citizen or resident living lawfully and permanently in New Zealand.

You may be granted residence if you are:

◆ the parent of an adult child 17 years or over who is a New Zealand citizen or resident who sponsors your application; and

◆ the 'centre of gravity' of your family is in New Zealand.

Note: Grandparents and legal guardians are also considered as parents in some situations.

'Centre of gravity'
The 'centre of gravity' of your family is in New Zealand if either:

◆ the principal applicant parent has no dependent children, and
◆ the number of their adult children lawfully and permanently in New Zealand is equal to or greater than those lawfully and permanently in any other single country, including the country in which the principal applicant is lawfully and permanently; or
◆ all of their adult children are living lawfully and permanently outside the principal applicant's home country; or
◆ the principal applicant parent has dependent children; and
  – the number of their adult children lawfully and permanently in New Zealand is equal to or greater than those lawfully and permanently in any other single country, including the country in which the principal applicant parent is lawfully and permanently; and
  – the number of their dependent children is equal to or fewer than, the number of their adult children who are lawfully and permanently in New Zealand.

Note: Under parent policy, 'children of the principal applicant' and the 'principal applicant's family' include:

♦ all biological or adopted children of the principal applicant; and

♦ any child of the principal applicant's partner (whether or not the partner is included in the application) if that child has lived as part of the principal applicant's family unit for a predominant period of the child's life between the time their relationship with the principal applicant began and when the child turned 17 years of age.

In addition, you and any family included in your application must meet health and character requirements.

Sponsorship requirements
♦ Your sponsor must:
   – be 17 years of age or over; **and**
   – be in New Zealand; **and**
   – be a New Zealand or Australian citizen or the holder of a current residence permit that is not subject to requirements under section 18A of the Immigration Act 1987; **and**
   – have been a New Zealand or Australian citizen and/or the holder of a residence permit or a returning resident's visa for at least three years immediately before the date your completed application is received by the NZIS; **and**
   – in each of the three 12-month portions within that three-year period, have spent a total of 184 days or more in New Zealand.

- Your sponsor will be responsible for:
  - ensuring that adequate accommodation in New Zealand is and continues to be available to you; and
  - if necessary, providing accommodation during the first 24 months of your residence in New Zealand; and
  - if necessary, providing financial support during the first 24 months of your residence in New Zealand.

Grandparents and legal guardians

A sponsor's legal guardian and their partner will be considered as parents under parent policy if both the sponsor's parents died before the sponsor attained the age of 20 years and the legal guardian had custody of the sponsor and the right to control the sponsor's upbringing before the sponsor attained the age of 20 years.

A sponsor's grandparent and their partner will be considered as parents under parent policy if both the sponsor's parents are deceased. Only one grandparent and their partner may be sponsored under parent policy.

In the context of parent policy where the principal applicant is a legal guardian, children of the principal applicant and the principal applicant's family include:

- the New Zealand citizen or resident sponsor; and
- all biological and adopted children of the principal applicant; and
- any children for whom they are or were legal guardians; and

- any child of the principal applicant's partner (whether or not the partner is included in the application) if that child has lived as part of the principal applicant's family unit for a predominant period of the child's life between the time their relationship with the principal applicant began and when the child turned 17 years of age.

In the context of parent policy where the principal applicant is a grandparent, children of the principal applicant and the principal applicant's family include:

- the New Zealand citizen or resident sponsor; and
- all biological and adopted children of the principal applicant; and
- any child of the principal applicant's partner (whether or not the partner is included in the application), if that child has lived as part of the principal applicant's family unit for a predominant period of the child's life between the time their relationship with the principal applicant began and when the child turned 17 years of age.

Sibling or adult child

You may be granted residence under this policy if you have a New Zealand citizen or resident parent, brother or sister who is living in New Zealand and who sponsors your application, and you have no other siblings or parents who are living lawfully and permanently in the same country in which you are living lawfully and permanently, and you have an acceptable offer of employment in New Zealand.

In addition, you must meet health and character requirements.

Sponsorship requirements
Your sponsor must:

◆ be 17 years of age or over; and
◆ be in New Zealand; and
◆ be a New Zealand or Australian citizen or the holder of a current residence permit that is not subject to requirements under s18A of the Immigration Act 1987; and
◆ have been a New Zealand or Australian citizen and/or the holder of a residence permit or a returning resident's visa for at least three years immediately before the date that a completed application is received by the NZIS; and
◆ in each of the three 12-month portions within that three-year period, have spent a total of 184 days or more in New Zealand.

Your sponsor must undertake to ensure that financial support and accommodation is provided to you, if necessary, for at least the first 24 months of your residence in New Zealand.

Acceptable offers of employment
Offers of employment are acceptable if they are:

◆ for ongoing employment with a single employer (ongoing employment is permanent, or indefinite, or for a stated term of at least 12 months with an option for the employee of further terms); or

♦ for one or more contracts totalling at least six months, if you have provided evidence of having had at least two years of contract work; and

♦ for full-time employment (that is, it amounts to, on average, at least 30 hours per week); and

♦ current at the time your application is assessed and at the time that you are granted residence, genuine and for a position that is paid by salary or wages (positions of self-employment, payment by commission and/or retainer are not acceptable); and

♦ accompanied by evidence of full or provisional registration, if full or provisional registration is required by law to take up the offer; and

♦ compliant with all relevant employment law in force in New Zealand.

Note: Compliance with relevant New Zealand employment law includes:

♦ a written employment agreement that contains the necessary statutory specified terms and conditions

♦ paying employees no less than the appropriate adult or youth minimum wage

♦ meeting holiday and special leave requirements or other minimum statutory criteria

♦ meeting occupational safety and health obligations.

Minimum income requirement

If you are including dependent children in your application you will also have to show that you will meet a minimum income requirement in New Zealand, to ensure that you can support yourself and your dependants if you come to New Zealand.

If your partner included in your application also has an offer of employment in New Zealand, their wage or salary can be taken into account when assessing whether you will meet the minimum income requirement.

Your partner's offer of employment must be an acceptable offer of employment (see Acceptable offers of employment, page 71), but does not have to be for full-time employment.

Number of dependent children	Total family income per year
1	NZ$30,946
2	NZ$36,493
3	NZ$42,040
4 or more	NZ$47,586

Dependent child
You may be granted residence under this policy if:

- you are aged 17 to 24 years; and
- you are single; and
- you have no children of your own; and
- you are totally or substantially reliant on an adult for financial support (whether or not that adult is your parent and whether or not you are living with that adult); and
- your parent(s) are lawfully and permanently in New Zealand.

or

- you are aged 16 or younger; and
- you are single; and
- you are totally or substantially reliant on an adult for financial support (whether or not that adult is your parent and whether or not you are living with that adult); and
- your parent(s) are lawfully and permanently in New Zealand.

Note: Your parents are lawfully and permanently in New Zealand if they are:

- citizens of New Zealand; or
- holders of New Zealand residence permits; or
- holders of current New Zealand returning resident's visas; or
- citizens of Australia; and
- actually residing in New Zealand.

You must also:

- have been born or adopted before your parents applied for residence, and been declared on your parents' application for residence; or
- have been born after your parents applied for residence; or
- have been adopted by your parents as a result of a New Zealand adoption or an overseas adoption recognised under New Zealand law.

Custody or visitation rights
If you are under 16 years of age and you have a parent

living outside New Zealand, your parent in New Zealand must provide evidence that custody or visitation rights of the parent living outside New Zealand would not be breached by you coming to live in New Zealand. In addition, you must meet health and character requirements.

Family Quota Category

The objective of the Family Quota Category is to strengthen families and communities by providing New Zealand citizens and residents with an opportunity to sponsor family members who do not qualify for residence under any other category of government residence policy.

The Family Quota Category allows for a quota of people each year to be chosen by ballot to be considered for residence in New Zealand. The number of places available under the Family Quota Category is announced by the Minister of Immigration each year.

You may lodge a full application for residence under this category only if your sponsor's registration is drawn from the pool (see below).

You may be granted residence under the Family Quota Category, if:

◆ you are sponsored by your adult child, adult grand-child, adult sibling or parent; and you are not eligible for residence in New Zealand under any other category of government residence policy; and

* your application is made within six months of the NZIS's advice to your sponsor that the sponsor's registration has been drawn from the Family Quota Pool.

Sponsorship requirements
Your sponsor must:

* be 17 years of age or over; and
* be in New Zealand; and
* be a New Zealand or Australian citizen or the holder of a current residence permit that is not subject to requirements under section 18A of the Immigration Act 1987; and
* have been a New Zealand or Australian citizen and/or the holder of a residence permit or a returning resident's visa for at least three years immediately before the date they lodge their registration under the Family Quota Category; and
* in each of the three 12-month portions within that three-year period, have spent a total of 184 days or more in New Zealand.

Your sponsor must undertake to ensure financial support and accommodation is provided to you if necessary for at least the first 24 months of your residence in New Zealand.

Note: If in New Zealand, you must be lawfully in New Zealand and not subject to section 129U of the Immigration Act 1987 to both be included in a sponsor's registration and in order to lodge an application under the Family Quota Category following a successful pool draw.

Registering for the Family Quota Pool
There are no places available under the Family Quota in 2004 and no registration period will be held.

If your parent, adult grandchild, adult sibling or adult child meets the requirements for sponsors set out above, and wish to sponsor an application for residence for you under the Family Quota Category, they must lodge a registration in the Family Quota Category Pool.

If your sponsor's registration is received within the registration period, their registration will be entered into the registration pool unless the registration is disqualified.

Your sponsor must pay a fee for registration (see the leaflet *New Zealand Immigration's Guide to Fees NZIS 1028*). If their registration is not successful in the Family Quota Category Pool draw, that fee will not be refunded.

Disqualification of registrations
If your sponsor lodges more than one registration during the registration period, all their registrations will be disqualified.

If two or more registrations are lodged for you (or any of your family members included in the registration) within one registration period, all of those registrations will be disqualified.

If you (or any of your family members included in the registration) have a residence application under any other category of government residence policy under consideration by the NZIS at the date your sponsor's registration is lodged, the registration will be disqualified.

If, at the time your sponsor lodges their registration, you (or any of your family members included in the registration) are unlawfully in New Zealand or subject to section 129U of the Immigration Act 1987 (concerning refugee status claimants), the registration will be disqualified.

Including family members in registrations
If you have a partner and/or dependent children, all of those people must be included in your sponsor's registration.

If your sponsor's registration is successful in the pool draw, only your partner and/or dependent children included in the registration may be included in the resulting application for residence under the Family Quota Category.

If your partner and/or dependent children were eligible to be included in the registration but were not included, they cannot later be granted residence under the partnership or dependent child policies of Family Category.

WORK VISAS

General Work Policy

Approval in Principle
If you are outside New Zealand and the job a New Zealand employer wants to offer you is not for an occupation on the Occupational Shortages List your employer can request an Approval in Principle. This application should be made to their local NZIS branch. New Zealand employers requesting approval must provide:

- confirmation of whether or not the worker requires New Zealand registration; and
- if more than one, the number of temporary workers sought, and
- the names of suitable applicants if known; and
- evidence of genuine attempts to attract and recruit staff from within New Zealand, and the reasons why New Zealand applicants were;
  - not suitable, or
  - refused to perform the work, or
  - cannot be readily trained to do the work; and
- if required, evidence of past and future compliance with employment and immigration law.

An application fee is payable. The fee covers the cost of processing the Approval in Principle and is non-refundable. The NZIS will write directly to the New Zealand employer advising the result of their application for an Approval in Principle. You will need to apply for and obtain a work visa before you enter New Zealand. If your partner or dependent children accompany you, they should apply for a visitor or student visa, depending upon their situation. The 'Approval in Principle' must be provided with your application for a work visa or permit.

Occupational registration

In New Zealand registration is required by law in order to undertake employment as one of the following:

Architect	Medical practitioner
Barrister or solicitor	Medical radiation technologist
Cadastral Land Title Surveyor	Nurses and midwives
Chiropractor	Occupational therapist
Clinical dental technician	Optometrist
Dental technician	Pharmacist
Dentist	Physiotherapist
Dietician	Plumber, gas-fitter and drain-layer
Dispensing optician	Podiatrist
Electrical service technician	Psychologist
Electrician	Real estate agent
Enrolled nurse	Surveyor
Line mechanic	Teacher
Medical laboratory technologist	Veterinarian

STUDENTS

New Zealand welcomes students from all over the world. To study in New Zealand, you will need to apply for a visa or permit.

Do you need a student visa?

You will need a student visa if you are outside of New Zealand, and are coming to New Zealand to study full time for longer than three months. (Your partner and children who wish to accompany you may apply for a visitor or student visa.)

Potential students entering as visitors to New Zealand from visa-free countries may apply for a student permit once an educational institute has accepted them.

Guardians accompanying students to New Zealand
A parent or guardian of students enrolling in school years 1 to 13, or aged 17 years or younger, may be issued a guardian visa for the purpose of living with and caring for the student. If a stay longer than 12 months is required, your permit can be renewed for further 12-month periods as long as the student continues his or her studies, until that student reaches the age of 18 years.

A student visa is:

◆ an endorsement you need in your passport to facilitate your travel to New Zealand for the purpose of study; and
◆ an endorsement you need in your passport if you are in New Zealand and wish to travel overseas and return to New Zealand for the purpose of study; and
◆ an endorsement showing you have permission to travel to New Zealand and may be granted a student permit when you arrive; and
◆ able to be issued for a single (one journey) or multiple (more than one journey) entry.

A student permit is:

◆ an endorsement in your passport which allows you to study in New Zealand. It will state the expiry date and give the conditions of your permit.

The conditions of your student permit will include details about:

- your course of study; and
- the educational institution; and
- the location of the institution in New Zealand; and
- any other restrictions (such as not being allowed to work).

Your course of study and educational institution must be approved for foreign students. The educational institution will advise you if their courses are approved.

You may apply for permission to work under the following circumstances:

- to fulfil course requirements; or
- up to 15 hours per week for tertiary students undertaking a long-term course of study; or
- during the Christmas and New Year holiday period; or
- on completing your course of study; or
- as a postgraduate student.

Do you need a medical certificate?
You must be of an acceptable standard of health. This is to ensure that you are:

- not likely to be a danger to public health; and
- not likely to be a burden on the health services; and
- fit for the purposes of entry.

If you intend to study a course which is 24 months or longer you will need to provide a medical and X-ray certificate. Your medical and X-ray certificate must be less than three months old at the time your application is lodged.

Will I be screened for TB?
You will need to be screened for TB if:

◆ you are intending to stay in New Zealand for more than six months and the country stated in your passport is not included in the list below; or

◆ you are intending to stay in New Zealand for more than six months and in the last five years from the date of your application you have visited, and/or lived in, a country or countries that are not included in the list below and the combined total of time spent in the country or countries adds up to three months or more.

Australia, Austria, Belgium, Canada, Cyprus, Denmark, Finland, France, Germany, Iceland, Ireland, Israel, Italy, Liechtenstein, Luxembourg, Malta, Monaco, Netherlands, New Zealand, Norway, Puerto Rico, San Marino, Sweden, Switzerland, United Kingdom, United States of America, Vatican City.

Are police clearances required?
If you are 17 years of age and over and intend to stay in New Zealand for a total of more than two years, you must provide a police certificate to show you are of good character. In order to prove you are of good character, you must supply the following:

+ a police certificate from your country of citizenship; and
+ police certificates from any country you have lived for five years or more since reaching the age of 17 years.

Your police certificate must not be more than six months old at the time your application is lodged.

What medical cover can be expected?
Residents and people holding work permits for a stay of two years or more (and their dependent children) are eligible for publicly funded health and disability services. Other work permit holders, students, and visitor permit holders generally are not eligible.

People covered by New Zealand's Reciprocal Health Agreements with Australia and the United Kingdom are entitled to publicly funded health care for immediately necessary medical treatment only. It is therefore strongly recommended that you have comprehensive health insurance for the duration of your visit.

RETURNING RESIDENT'S VISA
If you are a permanent resident of New Zealand, and wish to leave New Zealand temporarily, you need a Returning Resident's Visa to continue your residence status when you return to New Zealand.

You need a Returning Resident's Visa if you:

+ hold a Residence Permit and wish to leave New Zealand temporarily; or

- have held a Residence Permit, are temporarily overseas, and wish to return to New Zealand; or
- are a New Zealand citizen travelling on the passport of another country and wish to return to New Zealand using that passport.

You do not need a Returning Resident's Visa if you are:

- a New Zealand citizen with a current New Zealand passport; or
- an Australian citizen with a current Australian passport; or
- an Australian resident with a current Australian Resident Return Visa.

The length of your Returning Resident's Visa will depend on when you were first granted residence and your demonstrated commitment to New Zealand over the two years immediately preceding your application for a Returning Resident's Visa.

Your commitment to New Zealand may be in the form of your:

- time spent in New Zealand; or
- tax status; or
- investment; or
- business; or
- employment and family links in New Zealand.

Returning Resident's Visa policies
- General Returning Resident's Visa policy which

applies to persons first granted residence after 30 October 1995; and

◆ Transitional Returning Resident's Visa policy which applies to persons first granted residence before 30 October 1995.

The General Returning Resident's Visa policy applies to the majority of people and is therefore covered on this page. For details on the Transitional Returning Resident's Visa policy, please refer to the *Guide for Returning Resident's Visas*.

Note: If you are eligible for a Returning Resident's Visa under both the Transitional and General Policy, you will be considered under the provision that is more favourable to you.

General Returning Resident's Visa Policy
If you were granted residence after 30 October 1995, then the following rules apply:

◆ **First Returning Resident's Visa**.
You are issued your first Returning Resident's Visa free of charge when you are granted residence. This Returning Resident's Visa is valid for two years from the date of your first Residence Permit.

◆ **Second and subsequent Returning Resident's Visa**.
Eligibility for a second and subsequent Returning Resident's Visa is generally dependent on the circumstances of the principal applicant of the original residence application. If you are the principal applicant and qualify for a Returning Resident's Visa, then

your family members included in the original residence application will also qualify for a Returning Resident's Visa of the same currency.

The length of your second and subsequent Returning Resident's Visa may be for:

◆ an indefinite period; or
◆ a 12-month period; or
◆ a 14-day period.

Indefinite Returning Resident's Visa
There are five ways to qualify for an Indefinite Returning Resident's Visa. In all five cases:

◆ you must not be subject to section 18A requirements; or
◆ if you are subject to section 18A requirements, have met those requirements; and
◆ have held a residence permit at a time which was a minimum of two years before the date your Returning Resident's Visa application is lodged.

1. **Significant period of time spent in New Zealand**.
   You must have held residence permits for a total of 184 days or more in each of the two 12-month portions of the 24 months immediately preceding your Returning Resident's Visa application.

2. **Tax residence status in New Zealand**.
   You must have held residence permits for a total of 41 days or more in each of the two 12-month portions of the 24 months immediately preceding your Returning

Resident's Visa application. In addition, you must be assessed by the Inland Revenue Department as having tax residence status for the 24 months immediately preceding your Returning Resident's Visa application.

3. **Investment in New Zealand**.
You must have been approved residence under the Business Investor Category and have maintained your investment in New Zealand for two years. Alternatively, if you have been approved residence other than under the Business Investor Category, you must have maintained an investment of NZ$1,000,000 or more in New Zealand for at least two years after the grant of your residence.

4. **Establishment of a business in New Zealand**.
You must have successfully established a business in New Zealand that has been trading successfully and benefiting New Zealand in some way for at least 12 months immediately preceding your Returning Resident's Visa application. You may have been approved residence under any category.

5. **Establishment of a base in New Zealand**.

   ◆ You must have held residence permits for a total of at least 41 days in the 12 months immediately preceding your Returning Resident's Visa application; and

   ◆ each and every member of your immediate family who was included in your application for residence has held residence permits for a total of at least 184 days in the 24 months immediately preceding your Returning Resident's Visa application; and either

- you own and maintain a family home in New Zealand (you must have purchased the family home within 12 months of the date you were initially granted a residence permit and you and/or members of your immediate family who were included in the application for residence occupy that property); or
- you have been engaged in full-time, genuine employment in New Zealand totalling at least nine months in the 24 months immediately preceding your Returning Resident's Visa application.

12-month Returning Resident's Visa

There are two ways to qualify for a 12-month Returning Resident's Visa. In both cases:

- you must not be subject to section 18A requirements; or
- if you are subject to section 18A requirements, have met those requirements; and
- have held a residence permit at a time which was a minimum of one year before the date your Returning Resident's Visa application is lodged.

1. **Period of time spent in New Zealand**.
   You must have held residence permits for a total of 184 days or more in at least one of the two 12-month portions of the 24 months immediately preceding your Returning Resident's Visa application.

2. **Tax residence status in New Zealand**.
   You must have held residence permits for a total of 41

days or more in at least one of the two 12-month portions of the 24 months immediately preceding your Returning Resident's Visa application. In addition, you must be assessed by the Inland Revenue Department as having tax residence status for 12 months in the 24 months immediately preceding your Returning Resident's Visa application.

14-day Returning Resident's Visa

You must hold a residence permit but do not need to meet the requirements for an indefinite or 12-month Returning Resident's Visa. Applicants who are not in New Zealand will not qualify for a 14-day Returning Resident's Visa.

Special Provisions for Returning Residents

There are two special Returning Resident's Visa provisions for:

1. **Partners of New Zealand citizens**.

   You may be issued with a further two-year Returning Resident's Visa if you are a partner of a New Zealand citizen and do not qualify for an indefinite Returning Resident's Visa. This is provided your New Zealand partner supports your application in writing and evidence of your ongoing relationship is submitted.

   An applicant making an application for a Returning Resident's Visa on the basis of being the partner of a New Zealand citizen or resident must provide:
   - evidence of their relationship with their New Zealand citizen or resident partner
   - evidence that their partnership is ongoing.

Dependents of a partner of a New Zealand citizen may be issued with a Returning Resident's Visa current for a period equivalent to that of the partner's, provided the dependent children were included in that partner's residence application.

Note: In the case where an applicant is reliant solely on being the partner of a New Zealand citizen or resident for the purposes of obtaining a Returning Resident's Visa, the onus of proving that their partnership is ongoing lies with the applicant and their partner.

2. **Residents seconded overseas as part of their New Zealand employment**.
You may be issued with a further two-year Returning Resident's Visa if you are seconded overseas as part of your New Zealand employment and do not qualify for an Indefinite Returning Resident's Visa. This is provided your New Zealand employer confirms in writing that you are required to remain overseas and you are still considered a New Zealand resident. You may renew your Returning Resident's Visa under this provision every two years, for up to a total of eight years stay outside New Zealand.

How to apply for a Returning Resident's Visa
You should apply to the nearest branch office or diplomatic or consular representative of the New Zealand Immigration Service. To make an application, you will need to supply all of the following:

◆ a fully completed Application for Returning Resident's

Visa form; and

* the correct visa fee (see *New Zealand Immigration's Guide to Fees*); and
* your current passport; and
* evidence that you hold, or have held (or are considered under section 44 of the Act to hold or have held) a residence permit; and
* evidence that you are eligible for a Returning Resident's Visa.

Note: The passports of all persons included in the application must be submitted with the Returning Resident's Visa application.

If your partner and children intend to travel overseas temporarily and return to New Zealand, they should obtain Returning Resident's Visas. Your partner and dependent children under 20 years of age do not need to complete separate application forms or pay separate fees if they are included in your application for a Returning Resident's Visa. Your family's Returning Resident's Visa will be made current for the same period as your (the principal applicant's) Returning Resident's Visa. Children 17 years of age or older who are not dependent and all children 20 years of age and over must make their own application for a Returning Resident's Visa and must pay a separate fee.

How to prove residence status

Acceptable evidence to prove your residence status includes:

- a current or expired passport or travel document endorsed with your New Zealand Residence Permit or previous Returning Resident's Visa; or
- the original letter you received when you were first granted permanent residence in New Zealand; or
- your New Zealand passport.

Note: If you arrived in New Zealand before 2 April 1974 and did not receive a Residence Permit, you must provide evidence that you arrived before this date and have lived in New Zealand or Australia continuously ever since.

Acceptable evidence which must all be dated in New Zealand before 2 April 1974 may include:

- a New Zealand driver's licence; or
- bank statements; or
- employment references; or
- New Zealand school reports; or
- marriage certificates; or
- any other evidence requested by the NZIS.

Can a Returning Resident's Visa be used for more than one overseas visit?
There is no limit on the number of times you can leave New Zealand if you have been granted a multiple entry Returning Resident's Visa. You must ensure that your Returning Resident's Visa is current when you travel.

What if I left New Zealand without a Returning Resident's Visa?
You will need to apply for a further Returning Resident's Visa at a New Zealand Immigration Service branch office or diplomatic or consular representative.

When you make your application, you will have to provide evidence that you were a lawful resident of New Zealand before your departure, and that you are entitled to a Returning Resident's Visa.

What if the Returning Resident's Visa expires before returning to New Zealand?
You will need to apply for a further Returning Resident's Visa at a New Zealand Immigration Service branch office or diplomatic or consular representative.

If you have not held a residence permit in the three months preceding your application, you will be required to meet both health and character requirements.

Could a Returning Resident's Visa be refused?
You could be refused a Returning Resident's Visa if you:

- have had your Residence Permit revoked; or
- have been deported from New Zealand; or
- are applying from outside New Zealand and have an expired Returning Resident's Visa; or
- left New Zealand without a Returning Resident's Visa.

If you are refused a further Returning Resident's Visa, you will have to reapply for residence in New Zealand. Your application will be considered under the residence policy current at the time that you make your application.

Approval for a new Residence Visa or Permit cannot be guaranteed, as policy may have changed since you were originally granted residence.

WORK TO RESIDENCE POLICY

The Work to Residence policy has four options that provide a pathway to gaining residence in New Zealand, beginning with a temporary work visa or work permit. The four options providing pathways to residence are:

1. Talent policy – employment with accredited employers.

2. Talent policy – for people with exceptional talent in a field of art, culture, or sport.

3. Priority Occupations List policy – employment in an occupation on the Priority Occupations List.

4. Business policy – long-term business visa/permit category.

How to qualify for a work visa or work permit under the Work to Residence policy

All applicants under the Work to Residence policy must meet lodgement, bona fide applicant, health, and character requirements. The key additional requirements which must be met to qualify for a work visa or work permit under each of the Work to Residence policies are set out below:

Talent (Accredited Employers) Work Policy
You may be eligible for a work visa or work permit under this policy if you:

◆ are aged 55 years or under; and
◆ have an offer of employment in New Zealand with an accredited employer which meets the requirements below; and

* have met, or are able to meet, any New Zealand registration requirements if registration is required to take up the employment offered.

Offers of employment from accredited employers must be:

* for employment in New Zealand; and
* for a period of at least 24 months; and
* for full-time employment (that is it amounts to, on average, at least 30 hours per week); and
* current at the time the NZIS assesses your application and at the time of issue of the visa and/or grant of the permit; and
* genuine; and
* for a position with a minimum base salary of NZ$45,000 per annum; and
* accompanied by evidence of full or provisional registration, or eligibility for such registration, if full or provisional registration is required by law to take up the offer; and
* compliant with all relevant employment law in New Zealand.

Talent (Arts, Culture and Sports) Work Policy
You may be eligible for a work visa or work permit under this policy if you:

* are aged 55 years or under; and
* satisfy the NZIS you have exceptional talent in a declared field of art, culture, or sport as described below; and

◆ are sponsored by a New Zealand organisation of
national repute in your declared field.

*What is considered to be 'exceptional talent in a field of
art, culture, or sport'?*
You will be considered to have exceptional talent in a field
of art, culture, or sport if you can satisfy the NZIS:

◆ you have an international reputation and record of
excellence in your declared field; and
◆ you are still prominent in that field; and
◆ your presence in New Zealand will enhance the quality
of New Zealand's accomplishments and participation
in that field of art, culture, or sport.

*What is considered to be an 'organisation of national
repute'?*
A New Zealand organisation of national repute is:

◆ a New Zealand organisation that has a nationally
recognised record of excellence in a field of art, culture,
or sport; or
◆ a New Zealand organisation that has a nationally
recognised record of excellence in fostering exceptional
talent in a field of art, culture, or sport.

Priority Occupations List Work Policy
You may be eligible for a work visa or work permit under
this policy if you:

◆ have an offer of employment in New Zealand in an
occupation that is included on the Priority Occupations List and that meets the specifications for that

occupation; and

♦ are suitably qualified by training and/or experience to undertake your offer of employment as well as meeting any specific requirements set out in the Priority Occupations List.

Offers of employment under Priority Occupations List Work policy must be:

♦ for employment in New Zealand; and
♦ for a period of at least 24 months; and
♦ for full-time employment (that is it amounts to, on average, at least 30 hours per week); and
♦ current at the time NZIS assesses your application and at the time of issue of the visa and/or grant of the permit; and
♦ genuine; and
♦ accompanied by evidence of full or provisional registration, or eligibility for such registration, if full or provisional registration is required by law to take up the offer; and
♦ compliant with all relevant employment law in New Zealand.

Business Policy – Long-Term Business Visa/Permit
You may apply for a work visa or work permit under this policy if you are a potential migrant interested in applying for residence under the Entrepreneur Category.

You may also apply under this policy if you are interested in establishing a business in New Zealand but do not wish to live permanently in New Zealand. The New Zealand

Immigration Service Business Migration Branch assesses all applications lodged under the Long-Term Business Visa/Permit category.

To qualify under the Long-Term Business Visa/Permit category policy, you must:

- have a satisfactory business plan; and
- have, in addition to investment capital, sufficient funds for your maintenance and accommodation and that of any non-principal applicants; and
- satisfy an NZIS business immigration specialist that you are genuinely interested in establishing a business in New Zealand.

In addition, you and any family included in your application must meet health and character requirements.

A business plan is a proposal to establish a specific business in New Zealand. This plan must include the following information, and be supported by appropriate documentation:

- an outline of your proposed business and its viability; and
- financial information (forecasts and financing options); and
- details of your business experience (including English language ability); and
- your knowledge of the New Zealand market.

(For more information about business plans, see pages 48–60.)

How long can I stay under Work to Residence policy?
If you are successful in applying under a Work to Residence policy you will be issued with a multiple work visa allowing the grant of a work permit current for the periods set out below:

◆ Talent (Accredited Employers) Work Policy: 30 months
◆ Talent (Arts, Culture and Sports) Work Policy: 30 months
◆ Priority Occupations List Policy: 30 months
◆ Business Policy – Long-term business visa/permit category: 36 months.

How to qualify for Residence under Work to Residence policy
You may be able to qualify for residence if you are the holder of a work visa and permit approved under one of the Work to Residence policies and can also meet normal residence policy requirements. The key requirements are set out below:

◆ **Talent (Accredited Employers) Residence Policy**. You will be eligible for residence under this policy if you:
   – have held a work visa or permit granted under the Talent (Accredited Employers) Work policy for at least 24 months; and
   – have been employed in New Zealand for a period of at least 24 months by an accredited employer; and

- have current employment in New Zealand with a minimum base salary of at least NZ$45,000 per annum.
- ◆ **Talent (Arts, Culture and Sports) Residence Policy**. You will be eligible for residence under this policy if you:
  - have held a work visa or permit granted under the Talent (Arts, Culture and Sports) Work Policy for at least 24 months; and
  - have been actively engaged in your declared field of art, culture, or sport throughout a period of 24 months in New Zealand; and
  - are still prominent in that field of art, culture, or sport; and
  - have sponsorship by an organisation of national repute in your declared field (see 'What is considered to be an "organisation of national repute?"', page 97); and
  - you (and any partner or dependent children included in your application) have not, since the grant of your permit under this policy, applied for or been granted welfare assistance under the New Zealand Social Security Act 1964.

- ◆ **Priority Occupations List Residence Policy**. You may be eligible for residence if you:
  - are aged 55 years or under; and
  - have held a work visa and permit under this policy for at least 24 months; and
  - have been employed in New Zealand in an occupation included on the Priority Occupations List throughout a period of at least 24 months; and
  - have employment in New Zealand with a minimum base salary of at least NZ$45,000 per annum that is

either:

1. in the same occupation that enabled you to obtain a work visa and permit under this policy, or
2. in an occupation on the Priority Occupations List current at the time you apply for residence.

- **Business Policy – Long-Term Business Visa and Permit Category**. The New Zealand Immigration Service Business Migration Branch assesses all applications lodged under the Business Policy – Entrepreneur category. You may be eligible for residence under the Business Policy – Entrepreneur category if you can demonstrate that:
  - you have established a business in New Zealand; and
  - your business is benefiting New Zealand in some way.

New Zealand at a Glance

USEFUL INFORMATION

Phone numbers

- Fire, police, ambulance emergencies: phone 111 for fire, police or ambulance and do not hang up as you will be required to give information.
- International operators: dial 0170.
- International directory assistance: dial 0172.
- Local operator: dial 010.
- New Zealand directory assistance: dial 018.
- Local calls are free.
- All parts of New Zealand operate in the same time zone.

Density of population

The density is 14 people per km squared compared to 244.1 in the UK.

The population is at an all time high of 4 million.

Exports

Main exports are wool, food, dairy products, wood and paper products.

Average salaries and house prices

◆ Average annual salary is NZ$41,300, enhanced by the cheap cost of living.

◆ Average national house price is NZ$183,000.

Geography

New Zealand is 1,600 kilometres or 1,000 miles in length. The North Island area is 115,000 square kilometres, and South Island is 151,000 square kilometres. Stewart Island, located just south of the South Island, is 1,700 square kilometres. The total land area is 271,000 square kilometres. New Zealand is situated 2,250 kilometres east of Australia and 10,400 kilometres south west of North America.

Climate

Mid-season maximum average daily temperatures in degrees Celsius, rainfall averages (mm) and sunshine hours per year are shown below.

Location	Summer	Winter	Rainfall	Sunshine
North Island				
Bay of Islands	25C (77F)	15C (60F)	1648	2020
Auckland	23C (73F)	14C (57F)	1268	2140
Rotorua	23C (73F)	12C (54F)	1511	1940
Napier	24C (75F)	13C (55F)	780	2270
Wellington	20C (68F)	11C (52F)	1271	2020

South Island

Nelson	22C (72F)	12C (54F)	999	2410
Christchurch	22C (72F)	12C (54F)	658	1990
Queenstown	22C (72F)	8C (46F)	849	1940
Dunedin	19C (66F)	10C (50F)	772	1700
Invercargill	18C (65F)	9C (49F)	1042	1630

National annual public holidays

New Years Day and 2 January
Waitangi Day, 6 February
Good Friday
Easter Monday
Anzac Day, 25 April
Queen's Birthday is celebrated on the first Monday in June
Labour Day is celebrated on the fourth Monday in October
Christmas Day 25 December
Boxing Day 26 December

Regional holidays (Anniversary Days)

Wellington	22 February
Northland	29 February
Auckland	29 February
Taranaki	8 March
Hawke's Bay	17 October
Nelson	1 February
Otago	23 March
Southland	23 March
Marlborough	1 December
Westland	1 December
Canterbury	16 December

Health and safety

◆ Vaccinations are not required to enter New Zealand. However, if a rash, fever and chills, diarrhoea, vomiting or any feeling of being unwell occurs you must see a doctor and advise them that you have just arrived from overseas.

◆ Visitors to New Zealand are advised to arrange their own medical insurance as public and private medical/ hospital services are not free. There is a very high standard of treatment and care.

◆ Accident cover is provided free of charge for personal injury. Visitors cannot claim damages in the New Zealand Courts therefore it is recommended that your travel insurance policy covers accidents.

◆ Emergency services are available through most hotels and motels. There will be a charge and it is again recommended that travel insurance covers all emergencies.

◆ Chemists (drugstores) are open normal hours and will display an alternative if after hours.

◆ There are no snakes or dangerous wild animals in New Zealand. The only poisonous insect is the now very rare Katipo spider.

◆ Travel safely and take every precaution to protect yourself, family and your belongings from the trauma of petty crime or a more serious offence.

◆ Always lock your car and ensure nothing is left inside.

◆ Do not leave luggage and bags unattended and use hotel safes. Make sure you have comprehensive insurance cover.

◆ Make sure that you and your family wear sunscreen, hats and have protection from the sun which can be very fierce. High-burn times are identified daily on radio.

Finance and business information

◆ Business hours are mainly 9am to 5pm.

◆ There are no restrictions to the amount of foreign money taken in or out of the country.

◆ All major credit cards and travellers cheques are accepted.

◆ Banks are open Monday to Friday from 9am to 4.30pm.

◆ Automated teller machines (ATM) are widely available at banks, in shopping centres/malls and on main shopping streets. You will require a PIN (personal identification number) from your bank to use these. The ANZ Bank is open in some city centres on Saturdays from 10am to 2pm and the ASB Bank has a seven-day banking service in major cities and tourist centres from 10am to 4.30pm.

◆ Internet banking is also widely available.

◆ New Zealand Post shops are open 9am to 5pm Monday to Friday. Some postal shops are open on Saturdays between 9am and noon.

◆ The New Zealand dollar offers a very favourable

exchange rate for those with the English pound or American/Australian dollar.

♦ Foreign currency can be easily exchanged at banks and foreign exchange kiosks in most cities and at the international airports. It does pay to compare rates as they will differ between the major institutions. All major credit cards are accepted.

General information

♦ English is the most spoken language in New Zealand. Maori is officially recognised.

♦ Visiting drivers will average approximately 55–64 kilometres per hour.

♦ Taxis operate 24 hours a day and can be contacted by phone or from stands.

♦ Buses for commuters operate regularly on time-tabled routes with fares based on the distance or number of sections travelled.

♦ Passports must be valid for at least three months beyond the intended date of departure of all visitors to New Zealand.

♦ Smoking is banned in New Zealand on most public transport, including airlines, and in public places like shopping malls and meeting rooms.

♦ Electricity is supplied at 230/240 volts, 50 hertz. Most hotels provide 110 voltac sockets for electric razors.

- Tipping and service charges – New Zealanders do not expect a tip for normal service, even in bars and restaurants. However if you want to leave a tip, it will be much appreciated but not expected. Service charges and gratuities are not added to hotel or restaurant bills.

- Tougher laws have been introduced giving the police more power in response to the threat of terrorist attacks with penalties of up to ten years imprisonment or a NZ$500,000 fine.

5 Government

New Zealand is a constitutional monarchy and a modern parliamentary democracy with a single legislature, the House of Representatives. The Governor General, who is appointed every five years, is politically neutral and resident in New Zealand. He or she carries out the public responsibilities of the Crown and represents the reigning British Monarch who, although constitutional head of state, has no active role in government.

In 1993, New Zealand adopted MMP (mixed member proportional representation) based on the German electoral system. The 120 members of Parliament are elected every three years either as electorate or list MPs. The electoral process for electorate MPs follows the traditional Westminster 'first past the post' system. List MPs do not contest a particular electorate, but are first selected as candidates by their political party. They are then appointed on the basis of their party's proportion of the national vote. There are seven Maori and 62 general electorates with the remaining 51 seats (the list MPs) allocated to parties according to their proportion of the national votes. As a result of the votes there may be a majority or minority government or a majority coalition government.

The Prime Minister leads the party or coalition which has majority support in the House of Representatives. Central Government is based in Wellington. The Cabinet is the decision-making hub of government which develops new laws, allocates money and makes policy decisions, comprises ministers of the Crown (who must be MPs) and is headed by the Prime Minister, who administers the country.

The state sector or public service is made up of government departments, ministries, crown entities and State Owned Enterprises (SOEs). SOEs operate as competitive, commercial businesses, but are owned by the government. Each SOE is registered as a public company and is bound by the Companies Act with two shareholding Ministers who are responsible to Parliament, appoint directors, monitor performance and set dividend levels. Crown Entities, like the Tourism Board, are uncompetitive, have their own governing legislation and are controlled, although separate by law, by the crown. The Budget or government's annual financial plan runs from 1 July to 30 June.

LOCAL GOVERNMENT

The two levels of local government consist of regional councils and city/district councils. The 12 regional councils are responsible for:

* parks and reserves
* resource management
* harbour administration
* the supply of water
* civil defence
* land transport planning and co-ordination
* bio-security (pest and weed control).

The 59 district and city councils' responsibilities are environmental health and safety, which includes:

* building controls and civil defence
* their community's well-being and development
* resource management, land use planning, roads and transport
* sewerage
* water
* recreation and culture.

Local government elections are held every three years on the second Saturday in October and voting is by postal ballot. You can vote in local government elections only if you are a registered parliamentary elector. Electorates are known as 'constituencies' for regional councils and wards for district and city councils.

VOTING

The right to vote in New Zealand is not compulsory but residents must enrol in the Electoral Roll as an elector. To do this you will need to have resided in New Zealand continuously for at least 12 months and be a permanent resident. You also must be 18 years of age or older and have lived in your electorate for at least one month. The Electoral Roll is located at the New Zealand Post Shops.

Only Maori registered on the Maori Roll can vote in a Maori Electorate; all other nationalities/groups must register on the General Roll.

Two votes are cast by registered electors: one for the political party (Party Vote) and the other is a vote for a chosen candidate who is seeking to represent a local electorate (Electorate Vote). A party must receive at least five per cent of all Party Votes cast at the election to determine its share of the 120 Parliamentary seats or win at least one General or Maori Electorate. Put simply, if a Party wins 30% of the Party Vote it is entitled to a total of 36 MPs. If it has 21 Electorate MPs the Party is required to appoint 15 List MPs to make a total of 36.

There are two main parties, Labour, who formed a coalition with the leftist Alliance party, and the National party.

6 The Legal System

New Zealand has an independent judiciary and a common law system based on the British justice system. Barristers, solicitors and lawyers are members of New Zealand's single legal system, and those who have held a practising certificate for at least seven years are eligible for appointment as judges. Justices of the Peace usually witness legal documents like wills, insurance claims and statutory declarations and may assist District Courts in deciding traffic and minor criminal charges. JPs number 10,000 throughout New Zealand and can be contacted through *Yellow Pages* under 'Justices of the Peace'.

There are four levels of courts:

♦ District Courts are located throughout New Zealand and have extensive civil and criminal jurisdiction. Serious crimes like armed robbery and rape may be transferred from the High Court to the District Courts for trial.

- The High Court of New Zealand is made up of 36 judges and the Chief Justice (an appointment made by the Governor General on the advice of the Prime Minister), all of whom travel to 13 centres throughout the country. The High Court deals with major civil claims and crimes and hears appeals from lower courts and tribunals.

- The Court of Appeal consists of the Chief Justice, the President of the Court of Appeal and six other judges. As the highest appeal court in New Zealand its role is to reconcile conflicting court decisions by determining the law of the land.

- The Judicial Committee of the Privy Council (appellate jurisdiction only sits in London) but the government is currently looking at alternatives and may establish its own Supreme Court in 2004.

New Zealand has a number of specialist courts:

- The Employment Court deals with labour relations and work matters.

- Family Courts deal with areas like custody, parental access, the care and protection of children, divorce, adoption and protection orders.

- Youth Courts deal with offences committed by young children (14–17 years).

- The Maori Land Court and Maori Appellate Court deals with matters relating to Maori land.

◆ The Environment Court deals with resource management, planning and development matters.

There are more than 100 authorities, tribunals and boards that deal with matters ranging from taxation, censorship, employment and tenancy. Jury service is mandatory if you are selected at random from the Electoral Roll. For this very important community service you need to be aged between 20 and 65 and you will probably be required to hear a criminal case. You can be excused from jury service if you have a very good reason, such as childcare responsibilities or a permanent disability. There is a minimal payment to cover costs and most employers are required to allow you the time to attend jury service. You may be exempt if you have served within the last two years.

GETTING LEGAL HELP

Most lawyers are qualified both as barristers and solicitors, but tend not to work in both capacities. Barristers deal with court work and solicitors with other legal work that does not require them to act for their clients in court. Lawyers provide independent advice and treat all their business and clients affairs with confidentiality. They are generally employed to:

◆ provide advice on legal rights
◆ check legal documents
◆ assist with immigration applications
◆ prepare rental and lease agreements
◆ provide conveyancing services for properties and businesses
◆ draft wills

- undertake divorce proceedings
- provide representation in matters involving the police
- arrange redress in cases of fraud or misrepresentation.

Their fees vary widely. It is best to obtain an estimate before engaging the services of a lawyer, barrister or solicitor. Free legal aid may be available, but may need to be repaid.

The Office of the Ombudsman is an independent agency whose main function is to assist citizens with complaints about local or central government. There is no fee for this service.

The Human Rights Commission is an independent body responsible for investigating complaints of a human rights nature, like discrimination, dispute resolution and eliminating illegal and unfair practices.

7
Working in New Zealand

CAREER PROSPECTS

With a clean and safe environment, moderate climate, affordable housing, a low density population to land area, New Zealand consistently rates as one of the best places to live in the world.

New Zealand was the first country in the world to adopt an eight-hour working day, and is a sophisticated and modern, highly technical, advanced western nation. It also operates in a competitive time zone, as it is the first OECD country to wake up each day and there is a distinct time-driven advantage for businesses to locate or invest in New Zealand.

Because of the isolation of this small remote country and a diminutive enthusiastic population that emulates the demographics of larger markets, New Zealand is an excellent place for cost-efficient trials, and the scrutiny of new ideas and systems like Eftpos and Internet banking. Major companies testing the market with new products are Ericsson, Vodafone, BMW and IBM. New technologies such as various mobile phones, e-commerce purchasing and Internet use were all tested in New Zealand before being released onto the world market. Also clinical trials of new biomedical products are undertaken by global companies who are clustering in New Zealand to research, develop technology and collaborate on commercial ventures.

Major industries, especially tourism, are located throughout New Zealand, but some regions are better suited to industries like viticulture and agriculture.

- The mineral-rich soils, warm climate and sheltered waters of Northland have contributed to the forestry, dairy, fruit, mining, cement and boat-building industries.

- Auckland is the base for 40% of New Zealand's manufacturing industries and 45% of New Zealand's wholesaleing infrastructure. There are also viticulture, education and service industries.

- Waikato, Bay of Plenty is a centre of dairy, forestry, pulp and paper processing, horse breeding, horticulture and floriculture, food processing, mining, and scientific and industrial research and development.

- Hawkes Bay, Gisborne is similar to the Waikato.

- Manawatu, Wanganui and Taranaki are similar to Waikato, plus oil, gas and petrochemical production.

- Wellington, the capital city is a centre of government, finance, education, film and television, information technology and telecommunications, and secondary processing.

- Nelson, Marlborough, and the West Coast is known for viticulture, horticulture, fishing, seafood, food processing, forestry, wood processing and mining.

- Canterbury is renowned for the electronics, telecommunications and software development industries, farming, viticulture and horticulture, also research and development, education and manufacturing.

- Otago and Southland at the bottom of the South Island has healthy farming, fishing and seafood, forestry and wood processing, farming, education, engineering and manufacturing industries.

However, because New Zealand occupies only a miniscule part of the world and plays a tiny role in the world market, finding work can very challenging in this competitive environment.

PLANNING AHEAD

The ideal situation is to start planning at least six to twelve months before you leave and organise a good employer who will sponsor you into a position on arrival. If, on arrival, there is not a job for you, even though you may be highly qualified, be prepared for a period of six months or more to find suitable employment. You may have to settle for a less senior position initially, but the benefit is that you will be accruing work experience, a prime requisite for most employment. It may take up to a year to fully adjust to the cut and thrust of a new way of life and establish yourself in a suitable position.

It is important to check that your qualifications are appropriate to New Zealand requirements before you move. NZQA, the New Zealand Qualifications Authority will assist you by assessing the relevance of your skills compared to similar New Zealand qualifications and determine whether your overseas qualifications meet New Zealand standards. The NZQA's decision is not binding to employers, educational institutions or professional bodies although the assessments are officially recognised. However, you may be required to undertake extra study if your qualifications do not meet the necessary standards. A fee is charged for this service which may take 8–10 weeks, so you will need to allow plenty of time.

Contact www.nzqa.govt.nz for more information or send for their education booklet.

FINDING A JOB

Seventy per cent of all positions available in New Zealand are not advertised, so networking is a valuable tool in securing a job. Join any group – Rotary, Chamber of Commerce, Lions, your children's school committee or sporting and interest groups like tennis or sailing clubs – and speak to everybody that you meet or do business with – lawyer, real estate or insurance agents – about possible job opportunities.

The website www.careers.co.nz gives a guide to salaries and conditions, with jobs listed in alphabetical order, industry or interest areas. Salary details, training requirements and current market demand are also provided.

All the major daily and local newspapers have situations vacant columns. Monday, Wednesday and Saturday editions carry the most extensive job vacancy sections. Check the following websites:

◆ *The New Zealand Herald*: www.nzherald.co.nz the national newspaper,
◆ *The Dominion Post*: www.stuff.co.nz the Wellington daily
◆ *The Press* in the South Island: www.stuff.co.nz

and look in *Yellow Pages* for personnel, employment, recruitment and management consultants.

Most international placement and recruitment agencies that handle executive and professional management positions are represented in New Zealand. You do not have to pay an employment agency a fee and they will contact you when a suitable position becomes available. Keep in touch with them and build a relationship so that they think of you first for that plum position. Once you have provided them with your CV and relevant information they will handle the details of applying for a position.

Job vacancies
Job vacancies are listed in most professional and trade

journals (nursing, medical, accountants, legal, plumbers, etc).

Websites

www.regboards.co.nz
www.movetonz.govt.nz/BM/away/links/qualifications.htm
www.nzjobfind.com/browse/3:3.5.registration-boards.htm

Education career opportunities

The *Education Gazette* published by the Ministry of Education advertises positions available in primary and secondary schools and is available from www.edgazette.govt.nz.

Vacancies within universities and polytechnics are advertised in the major papers and are available on the websites of the various institutions, which are available under Education (see pages 161–163).

For primary and secondary school teaching positions visit www.teachnz.govt.nz.

Responding to an advertisement

To accompany your curriculum vitae you need to include a covering letter of application stating why you would be the best choice for the job, along with your contact details and a brief summary of your skills and experience relevant to the position. Your CV or professional résumé must be brief (one or two pages) and also provide your contact details (in case it is separated from the covering letter), your residence status and visa details, qualifications and computer skills, professional/trade skills, work experience and achievements.

Fluent English is essential. Your CV is very important, as it will sell you. It needs to be immaculate and up to date and must include your work history, references, hobbies and interests. If required, post or courier photocopies of your references and documents only. Later, when you are requested to attend an interview, you will also need to provide references, contact details for verbal referees (personal contacts are very important), and any academic or professional certificates that are relevant.

Applying for work

As it may take six months or more to secure a job, the earlier you start and the more experience and qualifications you have, the quicker the process. Trades and some professions (doctors, plumbers, etc.) may need to register before they can work in New Zealand. You will be advised if there is a waiting list and whether extra training is required.

DOCUMENTS AND PAPERWORK

You must bring original or certified (verified by a judge or Justice of Peace) documents of qualifications and each degree diploma or certificate. Official transcripts of subjects studied, including marks and grade, and a syllabus or course description of each qualification may also be required. Apprenticeship documents and evidence of trade employment and experience are necessary. If your documents are not in English, make sure you provide a certified translation. Birth and change of name (marriage) certificates are essential.

WAGES AND SALARIES

The good news is the figures for the September 2003 Labour Cost Index (LCI) and Quarterly Employment Survey (QES) figures show a strong growth in salary and wage rates (including overtime), accompanied by continued growth in the demand for labour, according to Statistics New Zealand. This is the largest rise since the December 1992 quarter increases and the annual wage rates remain at the highest level since the September 1997 quarter.

Depending on your employment agreement, the employment policies of the company you work for, your experience, qualifications, and the area in which you work, e.g. accountants tend to earn more than electricians, the amount you are paid will vary. Men usually earn more than women which unfortunately is the norm worldwide. Professionals' rates of pay are higher than those employed in the manufacturing and service industries. Also wage rates vary from city to city – currently Wellington has the highest income per capita.

See the website www.stats.govt.nz for more information.

Useful websites for finding work

www.nzjobs.to.go.to (or email jobs@acb.co.nz/) is a comprehensive job search centre that specialises in migrants. They will also assist in setting up bank accounts and offer a range of accommodation options.

www.hi-q.org.nz is a job-matching service for highly qualified immigrants.

www.newkiwis.co.nz finds work for migrants after they

have arrived in New Zealand.

www.careers.co.nz provides information on training courses, job applications, CVs and employment.

www.netfinder.co.nz and www.searchnz.co.nz are search engines for assistance with CV evaluation and interview coaching.

www.jobcafe.co.nz will find a job for you.

www.jobs-on-line.co.nz has national newspaper job advertisements.

www.jobuniverse.co.nz has a database of national and international jobs.

www.nzherald.co.nz/employment lists online jobs from New Zealand's largest daily newspaper.

www.netcheck.co.nz specialises in IT, management and upper level positions and also offers general positions.

www.nzjobs.co.nz offers many jobs in different areas of employment.

www.monster.co.nz has listings of jobs, career advice and interview tips.

www.seek.co.nz is a general employment site with company profiles and an online CV writing service.

www.jobs.govt.nz lists state sector job vacancies.

www.alljobs.co.nz lists job opportunities on a regional and national basis.

www.eeotrust.org.nz ensures equal employment opportunities for immigrants.

General websites

www.consumer.org.nz advises on consumer rights and prices of goods.

www.ubd.co.nz is a directory of over 156,000 businesses, 123,000 products and 302,000 trade suppliers.

www.directmoving.com is a specialist site that provides international comparisons of cost of living data.

www.yellowpages.co.nz is the telephone listings for New Zealand businesses.

www.etsa.govt.nz is a guide to vocational training courses and apprenticeships.

www.cab.org.nz, the Citizens Advice Bureau, which provides free advice and assistance on all areas from health, the law, your rights, education housing and personal issues.

www.union.org.nz gives all the listings of New Zealand Trade Unions.

Minimum wages

In New Zealand by law there is a set minimum wage rate if you are aged 16 years or older. Employment Agreements must comply with this law. The minimum wage rate is:

Youth aged 16–17 years	NZ$6.40 per hour before tax (gross)
	NZ$51.20 per eight-hour day
	NZ$256 per 40-hour week
Adult aged 18 years and over	NZ$8.00 per hour gross
	NZ$64.00 per eight-hour day
	NZ$320 per 40-hour week.

EMPLOYMENT CONTRACTS/AGREEMENTS AND THE LAW

All employers must offer their employees a collective or individual Employment Agreement written in plain English.

The Department of Labour or Employment Relations Service has a website and free phone for advice on any employment issues: www.ers.govt.nz, Tel: New Zealand

0800 800 863.

The main legal requirements are:

- Minimum wage for employees aged 16–17 or 18 years and older as above.
- Both males and females must be paid the same rate for the same job.
- Three weeks paid annual leave after one year (12 months) of employment.
- Eleven paid statutory or public holidays per year when these fall on days of the week that an employee would otherwise work.
- Five days of special leave (sick, domestic or bereavement leave) after six months' employment.
- Up to 12 months parental leave after 12 months employment.
- Leave for defence force volunteers.

The Agreement may also include conditions relating to:

- duties and responsibilities
- the term of the agreement
- pay rates, basis for pay, pay day, and method of payment, pay review and other payments
- hours of work
- holidays and other leave
- training
- health and safety
- an employer is able to reasonably request that an employee dress to a certain standard
- codes of conduct and company policies

- restraint of trade
- ending the Agreement.
- Resignation must comply with the conditions of the Agreement.
- Retirement – there is no set age and an individual cannot be forced into retirement because of age. New Zealand's National Superannuation Scheme entitles all to a pension at the age of 65. Residence requirements vary.
- Dismissal must be fair and for a valid reason. If an employee feels that they have been unfairly treated they may take legal action or a 'personal grievance' against the employer.
- Redundancy must be agreed by the employer, employee and/or their union and can be before or after the redundancy is announced.
- Contract renewal price (if not stated there are no automatic rights).

Contracts must include:

- effective personal grievance procedures
- effective dispute procedures
- expiry date for collective employment.

UNION MEMBERSHIP

Union membership is not compulsory and an employee cannot be differentiated from because of membership. Membership of a union means an employee is covered by the union's collective agreement. A non-member must negotiate his or her own Employment Agreement.

The Employment Relations Service has a website to provide up-to-date information on all aspects of employer/employee relationships: www.ers.govt.nz or New Zealand freephone 0800 800 863.

The law is always changing and personal criteria will differ. It is recommended that individuals seek relevant advice and clarification of their position on the above site.

Banking and Finance

BANKS

New Zealand's banking system is supervised by the Reserve Bank of New Zealand whose main function is to implement government monetary policy and register and supervise other banks. There is an open door on bank registration so currently there are four major trading banks plus others, making a total of 18 banks.

Banking in New Zealand is very competitive and there is a wide range of banks offering associated services like mortgages and insurances of every sort from car to house, travel, business and health. Conversely, mortgages are offered by other companies who are specialists in that area and will also offer you insurances as above. Brokers or independent advisors will recommend the best products for your requirements usually for a fee, and they also collect a fee from the product's company.

All financial service providers are required to explain their fees and there must be no hidden costs. If you are unsure about any information do not sign anything until you have a satisfactory explanation or something in writing that you can discuss and compare with other options.

You do not need to be a New Zealand resident to open a bank account and most banks will open an account in a few days. You need to provide your permanent address and an IRD number (see page 150 or visit website www.ird.govt.nz/business-info/(or personal) to avoid paying the higher rate of tax. Most banks offer an Internet service and 24 hour telephone access.

Contact details for the major banks
♦ ANZ – www.anz.co.nz.
♦ ASB – www.asbbank.co.nz.
♦ Bank of New Zealand – www.bnz.co.nz.
♦ www.kiwibank.co.nz.
♦ Taranaki Savings Bank – www.tsb.co.nz.
♦ Countrywide Bank – www.countrywide.co.nz.
♦ National Bank – www.nationalbank.co.nz.
♦ Westpac Trust – www.westpactrust.co.nz.
♦ www.yellowpages.co.nz/_new_zealand_banks.htm.
♦ www.bankdirect.co.nz (personal banking only).

ATMs
Automatic teller machines (ATMs) which dispense cash are available everywhere and you don't have to be a customer of that bank to use their machine, although there may be a charge. Eftpos (Electronic Fund Transfer at Point of Sale) is in common usage at most retail outlets. The money is automatically debited from your account as you swipe it or enter your PIN (personal identification

number). This system, first trialled by New Zealanders, helps to reduce credit card fraud.

INTEREST RATES

Interest rates have been low and fixed-term rates have been eased which has encouraged New Zealanders to borrow and invest more heavily in property at the expense of long-term savings. Banks want to attract borrowers seeking terms of one to three years.

Fixed interest rates range from:

One year	–	6.30–6.80 %
Two years	–	6.59–7.15%
Three years	–	6.70–7.35%.

Establishing a Business

GENERAL INFORMATION

New Zealand's economy is primed for long-term competitiveness and offers a stable and secure business environment. With no subsidies, free movement of capital, steady GDP growth, low inflation, falling debt, high capacity global links and the major leaders in telecommunications creating a virtual suburb, alongside excellent export networks, the opportunities to build a successful business are unlimited. New Zealand's major trading partners are Australia, USA, Japan, China and the Asian nations, which represents a massive market of enormous potential. An educated workforce complements the flexible and deregulated market place. New Zealand also currently enjoys the lowest worldwide average tariff rates and energy costs (NZ 8 cents/kwh for an average office electricity charge). There is no payroll, social service or superannuation tax, which means overheads (staffing costs) are less than Australia and the USA.

A small levy for ACC (Accident Compensation) provides a no-fault protection system for everyone. (Incentive programmes, which provide businesses with discounts for a good safety record are run by the ACC to reduce workplace injuries.) New Zealand has a complete range of life assurance and other insurance facilities. Customs agents, clearing houses and forwarding agents are readily available. Legal and accounting services are provided by a wide range of practitioners from sole traders through to multinational partnerships. They must all be a member of their national bodies, The New Zealand Law Society and The Institute of Chartered Accountants. New Zealand and Australia share a comprehensive free-trade agreement which gives New Zealand duty-free access to a potential trans-Tasman market of 20 million people.

New Zealand's company law regime has been extensively reformed with The Companies Act 1993 as the main legislation. A company must have a name, one or more shares, one or more shareholders and one or more directors. The name must be approved by The Registrar of Companies (this takes about 24 hours) and every company in New Zealand must:

- maintain a registered office as the official point of contact
- keep registers of shareholdings, directors and any charges over company property
- adhere to specified reporting requirements (mainly the Financial Reporting Act 1993).

Overseas companies can register or conduct business in New Zealand but may require consent from the Overseas Investment Commission and be required to provide audited financial statements. For more information visit their website at www.movetonz.govt.nz/Bml/away/doing-business/sub-regulation.htm.

EXPORTING TO NEW ZEALAND

Customs duty is payable on the entry of goods and the tariff system is based on the international Harmonised Commodity Description Coding System. Rates have steadily reduced over the last few years. Anti-dumping rules apply and GST is also payable on imports. There are no restrictions on overseas owners of intellectual property rights, licensing or franchising New Zealand businesses. Royalties are not subject to New Zealand's taxation laws.

◆ Overseas exporters are usually not disadvantaged against New Zealand producers and it is recommended that the domestic demand is not underestimated.

◆ Partnerships, joint ventures and trusts are regulated by the Partnership Act 1908 which is based on the British Law, but are not as well developed as contract or company law in the event of a dispute. A joint venture will require careful planning and monitoring. The advantage in the above lies in the combination of overseas capital and/or expertise, local market share, business networks or resource ownership.

Holding business investments through New Zealand trusts may offer the advantages of tax minimisation and flexibility, but may be complex and unconventional.

Establishing a New Zealand branch may have immediate taxation consequences and require permission from the Overseas Investment Commission. Consent may also have to be obtained from the Commerce Commission and overseas companies must register within ten working days of starting business in New Zealand. Also, audited branch and company financial statements must be filed with the Company Registrar each year. Legal compliance obligations expose the overseas head office, although it has full control over the New Zealand business, to the full extent of the branch's liabilities. Usually the investment is through a subsidiary company rather than a branch. Overseas companies can establish a subsidiary by:

◆ acquiring an existing trading company
◆ acquiring an existing non-trading or 'shell' company
◆ incorporating a company.

Requirements for establishing a subsidiary are similar to those of a branch, but the benefits are:

◆ a separate legal identity
◆ limited liability of shareholders
◆ perpetual succession
◆ individual powers and obligations.

The Overseas Investment Commission gives consent for overseas people who want to control or acquire 25% or more of:

◆ businesses or property worth more than NZ$50 million, land over five hectares and/or worth more than NZ$10 million

♦ land on off-shore islands

♦ land over 0.4 hectares that includes or adjoins sensitive areas like foreshores, lakes, reserves or historic sites.

There are no restrictions on foreign investors repatriating capital or income from New Zealand.

THREE BUSINESS STRUCTURES

1. A **Sole Trader** owns all the business assets and is totally responsible for all business debts, risks, and obligations.

2. **Companies**: any person (alone or with another) may apply for registration of a company under the Companies Act, 1993, which sets out the basic operating procedures in NZ.

3. **Business Partnerships**: an ordinary or special partner-ship can be established following the guidelines of the Partnership Act, 1908.

A company requires:

♦ a registered name
♦ one or more shares
♦ one or more shareholders with limited or unlimited liability for the company obligations
♦ one or more directors.

For more information visit www.companies.govt.nz.

STARTING A SMALL BUSINESS AND SELF-EMPLOYMENT

People with the skills to establish and manage a business in a competitive environment are very welcome in New Zealand. There is growth in small businesses and operations based at home utilising computer technology. If you are self employed it is essential to develop and maintain links with other businesses and people by joining local groups like the Chamber of Commerce, Rotary, Lions, Jaycees and various clubs such as rugby, sailing or tennis.

The following list will give you an idea of the areas that you need to research when starting a small business.

- First you need to be certain that you have the health, personal qualities and experience required to own and operate a business.

- You will need to be familiar with the legalities which guide business practices and standards (see below).

- You need to research and reassure yourself that your business concept is commercially viable. A written business plan is essential at this stage with projected cash flow analysis, break-even calculations and forward budgets.

- After completing the above, finances have to be planned and arranged. Some new businesses are able to borrow funds, which means that capital can be reserved. Be very careful at this stage and make sure you have good advice. The old adage, 'A fool and his money are easily parted' is as applicable in New Zealand as anywhere else in the world.

- Your accountant or professional business advisor will advise you which of the above company structures are most appropriate for your business. The decision will reflect the type of business, projected profitability, the financial status and relationships of those involved in the new venture.

- Your advisor will ensure that your business structure meets legal requirements, that your assets are protected, your tax minimised and that your business has the flexibility for new partners or investors to become involved if required.

- Location and premises are vital for most businesses. Remember that parking, visibility, and plenty of floor and passing traffic are essential for success. Do you require storage or delivery bays? Familiarise yourself with the surrounding competition and other businesses

- Enlist professional advice before entering into the lease agreement and ensure that your business can operate long term.

- Check with the local council for any by-laws, health department requirements and new roads or developments that may affect your business.

- Check with your accountant or the Inland Revenue to ascertain the taxes you need to pay: personal, company, ACC, GST, fringe benefits (perks of the job, e.g. a car), sales, rental, business and stamp and artists' royalties. Books need to be maintained daily and records kept for five years. For confidential tax advice contact the IRD on the following website www.ird.govt.nz.

- Register your business name.

- Contact an insurance broker or a recommended agent for life and general insurance policies for partners and management.

- Carefully select your staff and provide a written contract as detailed previously on pages 127–129. Clarify details, hours, holidays, leave, superannuation and safety. If purchasing a business, check ongoing training commitments, long-service leave and any other liabilities.

- Check whether you require computers or printed business documentation like invoices, statements, receipts and payslips. Initially, you may be able to use available business stationery or secretarial services.

- Decide whether your business requires vehicles, and if so, what sort. Decide if they will be leased or owned by the company. Check the taxation status, e.g. fringe benefit tax.

- Security of your premises and of cash or stock is paramount.

- Plan your marketing and advertising using data from your business plan – website, business cards, brochures, referrals, media, trade shows, vehicles, sales people, telemarketing and direct mail are all commonly used advertising.

- Decide what credit, terms of credit and debt services you will provide.

♦ Consider the communication and business technology you will use – photocopiers, two way radios, mobile phones, after-hours answer services and computers.

♦ To operate a small business successfully, you may require formal training to manage the accounting, marketing, staff selection, supervisory skills and inventory control. Contact the Small Business Enterprise Centres who specialise in helping small businesses and providing support.

♦ Check the credit system that you will be using and ensure that details and assistance for everyone providing or using credit, e.g. retailers and consumers, is available on your business website.

ESSENTIAL CONTACTS AND INFORMATION

Intellectual Property Protection

Intellectual property is protected through a mix of statutes and common law, which includes:

> The Fair Trading Act
> Companies Act
> Copyright Act
> Patents Act
> Designs Act
> Trade Marks Act
> Tort of Passing Off
> Tort of Breach of Confidence

Employer/employee protection

The Employment Relations Act 2000 provides equality for all employees in an adverse or multiracial society.

Contact the Department of Labour for information on employee/employer responsibilities on NZ freephone 0800 800 863 or visit the website www.ers.govt.nz.

Other relevant legislation

The Fair Trading Act 1986 encourages competition and protects the public from misleading and deceptive conduct and unfair trading practices.

The Resource Management Act 1991 ensures all activities comply with environmental policies.

The Treaty of Waitangi Act 1975 charges the Waitangi Tribunal with making recommendations on resolving Maori land claims. Recommendations can only be made if the land is held by the government, a State owned enterprise or was transferred with a restricted title.

The Commerce Act 1986 governs New Zealand's competition laws such as restrictive trade practises, merger regulation and price control.

The Consumer Guarantees Act 1993 means traders have to be responsible for guaranteeing the quality of the goods and services they supply.

The Building Act 1991 regulates the building industry.

The Securities Commission (Act 1978) investigates suspected insider trading and promotes regulatory practices within the capital investment market.

Statutes, in addition to the normal contract law, regulate consumer credit. For more information contact the Reserve Bank www.rbnz.govt.nz.

The Occupational Safety and Health (OSH) service is responsible for setting occupational safety and health standards. For more information visit www.osh.govt.nz.

The Health and Safety in Employment Act 1992 is designed to prevent harm to employees at work and relates to the duties of employers in that it:

* promotes excellence in health and safety management
* prescribes and imposes on employers duties to prevent harm to employees
* provides for the making of regulations and codes of practice relating to hazards to employees. It also covers the inspection of the workplace by government and medical practitioners, recording of accidents and penalties for non-compliance

The Smoke-free Environments Act requires every employer to have a written policy on smoking in the workplace which allows employees who do not smoke to be protected from exposure to tobacco smoke. All workplaces must have areas that are designated 'smoker' and that includes shared space, such as lifts or reception areas.

The Human Rights Commission (HRC) is an independent agency for investigating and resolving complaints about discrimination and other human rights issues. (An employee may fulfil cultural or religious dress requirements without being discriminated against.) The HRC website is www.hrc.govt.nz or New Zealand freephone 0800 4 496 877.

TEN WAYS FOR AN EMPLOYEE TO BE FIRED FROM WORK
1. Lie, steal, or defraud their employer.
2. Assault, punch, hit or push anyone.
3. Say 'no' to the boss.
4. Misuse email and/or the Internet.
5. Break the rules.
6. Behave badly out of work.
7. Harass a workmate.
8. Do their job badly.
9. Antagonise colleagues and clients.
10. Romantic liaison with a superior or competitor.

REGULATORY INSTITUTIONS
The **Commerce Commission, Securities Commission** and **Take-overs Panel** regulate business conduct in New Zealand. The Commerce Commission investigates misleading or unfair trading practices. For more information phone NZ 0800 94 3600. Or visit the website www.com-com.govt.nz.

The New Zealand Stock Exchange (NZSE) was established in 1981 and monitors the behaviour of listed issuers and administers the Listing Rules. To be listed on the New Zealand Stock Exchange a company must:

◆ have a market value of NZ$5 million

- have at least 500 public shareholders who, together, hold at least 25% of the securities of each listed class
- fully comply with NZSE disclosure and other ongoing obligations.

Once a company is listed it must comply with the rules that protect shareholders and investors as specified in the NZSE Listing Rules.

Security Exchanges. Shareholder members of the New Zealand Stock Exchange deal in listed securities plus a selection of overseas listings. The New Zealand share market is small, consisting of approximately 150 listed entities with a market capitalisation of NZ$72 billion. The top ten stocks dominate the market and account for over 58% of the total value.

BUSINESS ORGANISATIONS

The following details will assist you if you are entering a new business environment.

- The **Business Development Programme** (BIZ) provides government services to help the management skills and ability of small- to medium-sized businesses. National contacts are listed in the blue government pages in the front of the telephone book. www.biz.org.nz.

- **Industry New Zealand** is a government agency that provides practical advice, training and funding to help develop businesses and regions. www.moveontonz.govt.nz or www.industrytaskforces.govt.nz.

- **Technology New Zealand** promotes the adoption and

development of advanced technologies in the community. Research grants are available which focus on technical developments. www.technz.co.nz.

- **New Zealand Trade and Enterprise** provides assistance to exporters through a global and experienced network on export procedures, markets and market opportunities www.nzte.govt.nz

- **Economic Development Association of New Zealand** (EDANZ) provides a range of services for business immigrants. www.edannz.org.nz.

- **New Zealand Chambers of Commerce and Industry** are voluntary membership organisations for businesses to establish new contacts, mentors, advocacy and seek advice through social functions. www.chamberco.nz.

- **New Zealand Immigration Service**. The Business Migrant Liaison Unit provides free information and support for migrants setting up a new venture. www.movetonz.gov.nz.

Other sources of information
Statistics New Zealand – www.stats.gov.nz.
New Zealand Govt Online – www.govt.nz.
Investment NZ www.investnewzealand.govt.nz.

Please note that this is only a brief outline on the above and as the regulations and laws are complex and may change rapidly, you are advised to obtain professional advice before making a final decision to invest or undertake business in New Zealand.

GENERAL INFORMATION

Long-term international investors appreciate New Zealand's fair, broad-based, low-rate tax regime, a legacy of 10 years of reforms which dramatically reduced tax rates and doubled taxation agreements and limited the total amount of tax paid. There are no death duties and only minimal capital gains tax.

New Zealand led the world in recognising the value of intellectual property for depreciation purposes and offers 100% tax deductibility for research and development. Most investment in New Zealand does not require approval, but the Overseas Investment Commission (OIC) is the governing body when investments involve land, fishing quotas, values of NZ$50 million or over, or equity of more than 25% in a company.

New Zealand has individual double tax treaties, which override domestic law, with Australia, Japan, the United Kingdom and the United States. This provides for the allocation of taxation rules levied in both countries. Taxpayers in NZ are encouraged to make voluntary, accurate and honest returns. Assessments of income or losses are received after filing an income tax return. The Inland Revenue has the power to seize relevant documents and conduct random audits and searches of your premises – an event that can interrupt daily activities and be very distressing.

All residents are required to pay tax on all the income received, whether generated in New Zealand or overseas. You are a resident for taxable purposes if:

◆ You are in New Zealand for 183 days (not necessarily consecutive) over any 12-month period (this commences on your arrival).

◆ You have an 'enduring relationship' with New Zealand. This includes:
  1. owning or leasing property
  2. social ties, family living and education of children in New Zealand
  3. economic ties, bank accounts, life insurance, credit cards
  4. employment
  5. whether you receive pensions or any other payment.

The following income is taxed in New Zealand:

◆ New Zealand resident's worldwide income.
◆ Non-resident's income which is sourced in New Zealand.

- Income that falls into neither of the above, but is controlled by one or more New Zealand residents.

- Incomes of husband and wife are treated separately for tax purposes.
- Partnerships are not taxable, but individual partners are taxed on their state of partnership income.
- Trust income is taxed to either the trustees or the beneficiaries.
- Charitable organisations, government departments and Crown Agencies are exempt.
- There are also gift and stamp duties, nominal import tariffs and various excise duties mainly for alcohol and tobacco.

There is no capital gains tax in New Zealand. However, profits from disposing of personal property are taxed when:

- it is acquired for resale
- the business is dealing in such property
- there is a scheme with the aim of making a profit.

If you have a taxable activity, either individual or corporate, in New Zealand that creates income you will also need to be registered to pay Goods and Services Tax. To do this you will require an IRD number from the Inland Revenue, which only takes a few days to issue and is necessary to start a job or open a bank account. The New Zealand tax year is from 1 April to 31 March and employers deduct tax from salary and wages.

Banks and financial institutions deduct tax on interest as it is derived. Business income is calculated on an 'accruals' basis, not when the payment is actually received.

People who are working on commission such as real estate agents, do not pay tax on their income as it is earned, but are required to file a tax return by year end, 31 March. Usually the IRD will post you the necessary material to make returns with.

Personal and Company tax rates in New Zealand for year ending March 2003 are as follows:

Tax rate for individuals, sole traders and partners:

0–NZ$38,000	19.5%
NZ$38,001–NZ$60,000	33%
NZ$60,001 and over	39%

Companies are taxed at the company tax rate of 33%.

Visit www.ird.govt.nz for more information and request the business booklet. It also advisable to seek professional advice if you are unsure of the correct procedure or have other queries.

COMPANY TAXATION

Resident companies pay New Zealand income tax on their worldwide income on a 31 March year end. Non-resident companies only pay tax on income sourced in New Zealand, both at the rate of 33%. A company is so defined if the Head Office or centre of management is located or incorporated in New Zealand, or if the directors control the company in New Zealand.

♦ **Domestic Dividends** are usually taxed if the dividends are received from a New Zealand-resident company. If a shareholder is a New Zealand resident company, dividends from a company of the same status are exempt as long as the companies are part of a wholly owned group of companies and have the same balance date.

♦ **Tax losses** may be carried forward and offset against the taxable income for a future income year with some restrictions.

♦ **Tax loss** grouping provisions permit offsets where the same group of companies obtains the tax benefits of the loss offset. The **consolidation regime** is for New Zealand resident companies that are 100% commonly owned.

♦ **Qualifying Companies** (QC) that are New Zealand resident companies can choose to have the ability to access capital gains, made by the QC, free of tax, dependent on meeting established criteria. Interest deductability on borrowed money is possible if:
– it is payable while earning gross income; or
– it is necessarily payable in conducting a business for the purpose of deriving gross income; or
– it is payable by a group company on money borrowed to acquire shares in another group company. Intercompany charges allow a group company to charge another group company for

management support or similar services.

• The **imputation system** is where resident companies can pass onto resident shareholders imputation credits that reflect company tax paid.

• **Foreign Dividend Withholding Payments** (FDWP) are where foreign dividends paid to company shareholders are subject to the FDWP regime. Companies normally maintain a separate FDWP credit account. The new conduit regime may protect non-resident shareholders from New Zealand tax on foreign sourced income.

• **Repatriating profits** are royalties, dividends and interest subject to Non-Resident Withholding Tax (NRWT). The rates are:
   - fully imputed dividends – 15%
   - non-imputed – 30%
   - interest and royalties – 15%.
   These rates may be reduced if the recipient's country of residence has a double tax treaty with New Zealand.

• The **Foreign Investor Tax Credit** regime covers dividends paid to non-New Zealand resident shareholders and avoids double taxing corporate income sent to non-resident New Zealand residents.

• **Non-resident Contractors Withholding Tax** is imposed on:
   - payments for services performed in New Zealand by non-residents
   - non-residents who lease personal property in New Zealand.

- **Resident and Withholding Tax** is deducted at source from the gross interest and dividend payments at the rate of either 19.5% or 33% depending on the recipient's choice.

- **Provisional Tax** is paid in three instalments depending on the taxpayer's balance date. Interest is charged or credited on underpayments or overpayments. Direct and indirect taxes include a resident corporate rate of 33% and a top personal rate of 39% on incomes over NZ$60,000.

- **Goods and Services Tax (GST)** is a goods and services or consumption tax of 12.5% which excludes exports and financial services. Individuals and companies are required to register for GST if their business turnover exceeds, or will exceed, NZ$30,000 in a 12-month period. Regular returns need to be filed either every one, two or six months of the GST collected or to reclaim GST already paid.

- **Fringe Benefit Tax** is payable on business perks which may be part of an employment package, such as a company car, club membership or accommodation.

- **Provisional Tax** is an instalment payment system that is paid in three instalments depending on the taxpayer's balance date.

- **Accident Insurance (ACC)** is compulsory and the only provider of no-fault work injury and accident compensation for all employers, self-employed and private domestic workers. This means that most of your medical bills will be paid if you are injured as a result of criminal action, sports injury or a medical mistake.

Average premium rates per NZ$100 of payroll are:
self-employed – NZ$1.64
employer – NZ$1.16.
Contact the Accident Compensation Corporation website for more details www.acc.co.nz or www.acc.org.nz/injury-prevention

EMPLOYER'S OBLIGATIONS
PAYE (pay as you earn) must be deducted from employee wage or salary payments. Superannuation employers are able to claim tax on their contribution to a registered employee superannuation fund. Cash contributions are subject to a 33% withholding tax. Fringe Benefit Tax must be paid on non-cash benefits to employees.

Every business:

♦ requires an Inland Revenue (IRD) number
♦ must complete and send various tax return forms and make certain tax payments to the Inland Revenue each year
♦ keep sufficient records to substantiate annual returns and payments.

A business may also need to:

♦ deduct PAYE (pay as you earn) employees' tax
♦ charge GST to customers
♦ complete regular GST returns.

If a business is not registered it cannot charge or claim back GST. Some goods and services like rent from domestic accommodation and income from financial services are exempt from GST. The financial year is 1 April to 31 March and New Zealand residents must include income from all sources when completing the necessary annual tax returns. Expenses that can be deducted are:

◆ business overheads (e.g. rent, rates, power, stationery supplies and telephone costs)

◆ vehicle and transport and equipment costs for the business

◆ trading stock and material costs

◆ employee wages, but not those drawn as personal remuneration.

For further information about starting and managing a business, to make an appointment for free business advice and to obtain a copy of the Inland Revenue's free book, *Smart Business – an introductory guide for businesses* (code number IR320) visit the website, www.ird.govt.nz, and select 'information for businesses'. If calling from outside New Zealand phone 0064 4 471 1145 (Wellington) or if in New Zealand freephone number 0800 377 774.

PERSONAL TAX

New Zealand residents are taxed on their worldwide income on 31 March with returns due immediately on the following 7 June. Individuals employed short term and paid by overseas companies are subject to New Zealand income tax laws.

Personal tax rates that apply for resident and non-resident individuals are:

NZ$0 – NZ$38,000 – 19.5%
NZ$38,001 – NZ$60,000 – 33%
NZ$60,001 and above – 39%

Rebates are available and may include charitable donations and housekeeping, but the onus is on the individual to ascertain what is appropriate. It is advisable to consult an accountant or tax specialist.

TRUSTS

Qualifying trusts are taxed at 33% and trustee income is all income derived by a trustee.

For more information contact the Inland Revenue Department, www.ird.govt.nz, an accountant or a tax specialist.

Education

In 1816, New Zealand's first school was established at Rangihoua in the Bay Islands, North Island. It was a mission school and had a total of 35 pupils.

New Zealand's two official languages are English and Maori.

Parents or guardians are legally responsible for ensuring a child is enrolled and receives government-funded compulsory schooling from age six to 16 years. Education is free until the age of 19 or 21 mainly for students who require special education. Corporal punishment is against the law. Legislation decrees that every educational institution must treat a disabled student the same as an able-bodied student and offer special education for those with different needs.

CHOOSING A SCHOOL
Most students attend the state school that is closest to their home. Zoning rules apply to reduce overcrowding,

but exemptions can be made. Families are encouraged to visit schools and meet with the principal and staff before making their decision. Education Review Office reports are available free of charge from schools or at www.ero.govt.nz. Also available is *Choosing a School for a Five Year Old* and *Choosing a Secondary School.*

The school year begins with Term 1 at the end of January through to early April. Term 2 is from late April to the end of June. Term 3 runs from mid-July to late September with the fourth and last term commencing in mid-October to mid-December, when a six-week summer holiday is taken. The school week is Monday to Friday and usually starts at 9am, finishing at 3.00–3.30pm with morning and afternoon breaks and an hour for lunch. Class size is, on average, 30 students.

The main types of school (which may be religious or interdenominational) are as follows.

1. State school education is government funded and can be available to anyone under the age of 19. Uniforms, stationery and books usually have to be paid for and parents are often asked to make a donation or pay school fees.

2. Independent private schools are usually run by a board, charge fees and have to meet required educational standards.

3. Integrated state schools follow the state curriculum and charge fees. Previously private schools, they often have a central doctrine, usually Roman Catholic, Montessori or Rudolf Steiner.

4. There are 24 boarding schools, which operate mainly at the private secondary school level and 78 state and integrated schools with boarding facilities.

The Correspondence School teaches a full range of courses as does Home Based Schooling.

New Zealand's education system is divided into three main sectors:

1. Early childhood education – for children aged between two and a half and five years and primary school for children aged five to ten years. This includes kindergartens, childcare, kohanga reo (where Maori language, culture and values are taught) and Pacific Island language and playgroups. Kindergartens are often free, although a small donation is expected and parents may be asked to help out with fundraising or committee work. Some have waiting lists and it is advisable to enrol your child as soon as possible. Most have two sessions a day which focus on learning through play and social interaction.

    Care centres are licensed to take children under two years of age and usually open for eight or nine hours a day. Care is available full time or part time between 7.30am and 6.00pm with fully-trained staff present. Different daycare centres set fees at a weekly or hourly rate. Also Montessori and Rudolph Steiner schools are to be found in the main centres. Playcentres are run by parents with an emphasis on community and family involvement. Nannies are also available as well as home-based care where the child is looked after in the carer's home.

Early Childhood Development, a government agency, provides information on the range of childhood services available and monitors ratios of staff to children and class sizes. More information is available from The Citizens Advice Bureau, and Plunket (see page 223).

2. Compulsory sector. Most children receive schooling from the age of five at primary schools and are known as 'Juniors' or 'Primers' in years 1–3. The years 4–6 are referred to as 'Standards', years 7–8 are known as 'Forms 1 and 2' and the years 9–13 as 'Forms 3–7'.

Children in their seventh and eighth year (11–12-year-olds) may attend an intermediate school or college.

Schooling for age 12–13 on to 17–18 is referred to as secondary school, high school, college or grammar. Students are usually grouped in classes but may have different teachers in other rooms for each subject. Students may leave at 16 years or stay until 19 years of age. Most schools are co-educational or 'co-ed' (both sexes) although single-sex schools are available. Many schools enrol up to six months before the starting date, so it is advisable to enrol early.

Correspondence, home-based education and boarding schools are available. As a locum you can do home schooling without having to apply to the Education Department.

3. Tertiary and other adult education (see pages 164–167). For further information contact the following

websites:

- ◆ Early Childhood Development, for advice on early childhood services – www.acd.govt.nz.
- ◆ Education Review Office which provides quality assessments of schools and pre-schools
  – www.ero.govt.nz.
- ◆ Group Special Education which provides services for children and young people with special needs
  – www.ses.org.nz.

- ◆ Association of Colleges of Education in New Zealand gives details and links to the four colleges of education – www.acenz.ac.nz.
- ◆ The Association of Polytechnics in New Zealand provides information and contact details
  – www.apnz.ac.nz.
- ◆ The Open Polytechnic of New Zealand specialises in distance learning at tertiary level
  – www.topnz.ac.nz.

- ◆ Correspondence courses at all levels
  – www.correspondence.school.nz.
- ◆ Information on studying in New Zealand and contacts – www.educationnz.org.nz.
- ◆ EduSearch provides information on New Zealand's education system from pre-school to adult
  – www.edusearch.co.nz.
- ◆ Information for overseas students
  – www.myzcd.com.
- ◆ Independent guide to what is available from diving schools to tertiary institutions
  – www.piperpat.co.nz/nz/index.html.

- New Zealand Boarding Schools
  – www.boarding.org.nz.
- Information on 43 independent (private) schools
  – www.independentschools.org.nz.
- New Zealand Kindergartens Inc
  – www.nzkindergarten.org.nz.
- New Zealand Playcentre Federation
  – www.playcentre.org.nz.

THE CURRICULUM

The New Zealand curriculum identifies seven 'essential learning' areas:

- language
- mathematics
- science
- technology
- social sciences
- the arts
- health and physical well-being

which are further complemented by eight 'essential skills':

- communication
- numeracy
- information
- problem solving
- self-management and competitive
- social and co-operative
- physical
- work and study.

Each term, student progress reports are provided and parent-teacher evenings are held at most schools.

EXAMINATIONS

The National Certificate of Educational Achievement is made up of credits in each subject area, which are awarded for meeting pre-defined standards. Sixty per cent of the achievement standards are assessed externally with end-of-year examinations marked outside of the school by teachers. The balance is internally assessed. Eighty credits must be obtained with at least 60 from the relevant level.

♦ NCEA level 1 or year 11 (5th form) is comparable to British GCSE at grades A to E; United States or Canadian grade 10; Australian, Year 10 awards, School, Achievement and Junior Certificates.

♦ NCEA level 2 (year 12 or 6th form) is the equivalent to the United States or Canadian Grade 11.

♦ NCEA level 3 (year 13, 7th form) and (which has just replaced the Sixth Form Certificate) is awarded to students (year 12) who complete a one year approved course in one to six subjects, including English. For further information go to www.ncea.govt.nz.

♦ University Bursaries and Scholarship examinations of up to six subjects, are usually taken in year 13 or the final year, with a separate exam for each subject. A mark of over 86% or the top 4% of achievers are awarded a scholarship in an individual subject. Students may then be awarded an A or B Bursary dependant on total marks of 250 to 300 and may receive a small cash allowance.

TERTIARY EDUCATION

With most of the adult population literate, half of all students continue their study at one of New Zealand's eight universities or 22 polytechnics. Both provide three- or four-year degrees, offer a wide range of academic, vocational and professional courses and promote research. Short full-time and part-time courses are also available at polytechnics. There are three Maori tertiary institutions called wananga where learning is based on ahuatanga (Maori tradition) and tikanga (Maori custom). State tertiary institutions are 75% government funded. Fees vary from NZ$2,000 to NZ$20,000, depending on the course.

Students may also undertake teacher training at a college of education in Auckland, Wellington, Christchurch or Dunedin. For further information contact www.teachnz.govt.nz.

A wide range of courses is also offered at several thousand private training establishments throughout New Zealand, of which over 800 are registered with the NZ Qualifications Authority, which ensures they attain a recognisable standard.

Universities, websites and subjects offered

North Island

University of Auckland: www.auckland.ac.nz. Architecture, Planning, Engineering, Medicine, Optometry, Fine Arts, Law.

Auckland University of Technology: www.aut.ac.nz.

Health Studies, Tourism, Engineering, Communications, Hotel Management.

University of Waikato (Hamilton): www.waikato.ac.nz. Law, Maori Studies.

Massey University (Albany, north of Auckland, Palmerston North and Wellington): www.massey.ac.nz. Agriculture and Horticulture, Aviation Studies, Business Studies, Design, Food Technology, Social Sciences, Veterinary Science, also extra mural courses.

Victoria University (Wellington): www.vuw.ac.nz. Architecture, Design, Public Administration, Social Work, Law.

South Island

University of Canterbury (Christchurch):
    www.canterbury.ac.nz. Engineering, Forestry, Fine Arts, Journalism.

Lincoln University (near Christchurch):
    www.lincoln.ac.nz. Agriculture and Horticulture, Natural Resource Management.

University of Otago (in Dunedin): www.otago.ac.nz. Dentistry, Law, Medicine, Physical Education, Pharmacy, Surveying, Theology.

New Zealand has 22 polytechnics offering a wide range of academic, vocational and professional courses scheduled throughout the year. There are four colleges of education or teacher training colleges located in Auckland, Wellington, Christchurch and Dunedin. Waikato and Massey Universities also offer teacher training.

Entry levels for university require an A or B Bursary. Admittance is very competitive to some courses and only students with high standards of academic learning are accepted in those instances. Polytechnics may vary. Each tertiary institution has different entry requirements for overseas students these are available by contacting the relevant institution's website (see www.apnz.ac.nz). Intending students for all of the above should apply in September for the beginning of the first term in the following February of the new year.

Allowances may be available to students who hold the permanent resident status of a minimum two years residence through Study Link. The allowance is means tested. For further information contact www.winz.-govt.nz.

Where to Live

NORTH ISLAND

The Northland region, population 141,900 and historic cradle of New Zealand, has it all. Climate, million dollar views, lush pastures, lofty forests, and isolated spots where the surf pounds sandy beaches make it a very desirable and, in some areas, an expensive place to live. At Cape Reinga you can stand near the lighthouse and view boiling 10-metre-high waves in stormy weather where the South Pacific Ocean and Tasman Sea converge.

At low tide you can drive along 90 Mile Beach (which is really 116 kms) to Kaitaia, a good place to experience and learn more about Maori culture. Here Maori and Dalmatians have thriving communities. South of Kaitaia on the Hokianga Harbour where the fish and chips are great and fishing or gathering shellfish can easily be arranged, is Opononui. In the 1950s, this frontier town was made famous by 'Opo' the tame dolphin that stayed and played.

On the wild and untamed western side of the North Island's narrow neck is the Waipoua Forest. This, the largest remnant of New Zealand's northern extensive native kauri forests and proclaimed a sanctuary in 1952 after continued antagonism and public pressure, is full of spectacular giant kauris that reach up to form a wonderful canopy. There you can find Te Matua Ngahere, the Father of the Forest with a girth of over five metres, and which, at more than 4,000 years old, is probably the oldest rainforest tree on earth a staggering height of 51 metres is Tane Mahuta, God of the Forest.

On the sheltered eastern sunny coast is the historic, beautiful and tranquil Bay of Islands with picturesque Kerikeri at the northern end nestling amidst the orange groves. Paihia and Russell form the gateway to 150 islands scattered in a glassy sea – a boatie's dream, and across the water is historic Waitangi where the Treaty of Waitangi was signed in 1840. Heading south is Tutukaka, famed for deep-sea fishing and Whangarei, haven for yachts and a major city of 46,000 people. Popular for scuba-diving is the nearby marine reserve The Poor Knights Islands, that are rated as one of the top diving spots in the world.

Export, trade and investment opportunities are tourism, land, forestry (pine plantations and mills), boat building and horticulture. Websites for more information are:
www.nrc.co.nz
www.northland.co.nz
www.northland.org.nz.

Auckland, with a population of 1.291 million plus that is rapidly increasing because of a rising birthrate and immigration, is an aquatic playground with two harbours, a gulf full of islands, the highest density of pleasure boats in the world and a rugged West Coast. There are 48 dormant volcanoes, which make excellent vantage points on the long, sunny and often humid days of summer (best between January and April) for viewing the surrounding islands. Some, like the largest and very popular Waiheke Island (population 8000), offer homes for commuters and those wanting a weekend retreat.

Others like Tiritiri Matenga and Little Barrier are a sanctuary for birds and their native habitat while Rangitoto, a cone-shaped volcano dominates the Waitemata Harbour. Kelly Tarlton's Antarctic Encounter and Underwater World is situated adjacent to the harbour.

The Downtown Viaduct Harbour is usually full of large, international seagoing yachts with throngs of people enjoying the superb restaurants, boutiques, bars and hotels of the encircling village.

The new Britomart Train system, located in downtown Auckland will eventually help reduce some of the city's traffic congestion. An extra funding and governance package of NZ$1 billion is to be paid to Auckland over the next ten years to deal with the city's infrastructure problems. The thinking is that Auckland's success is pivotal to the economic and social well-being of the country.

Auckland's colourful tapestry of culture, cuisine and

sophisticated ways also embraces the world's largest Polynesian population and an increasing number of Asians (as those from Japan, China, Korea and Malaysia are known – those from India are known as Indians). The annual and free Concerts in the Park embrace the diversity of Auckland's cosmopolitan population. There is nothing better than experiencing the good-natured atmosphere of families enjoying a picnic whilst listening to Dame Kiri Te Kanawa's glorious voice, a massed choir or orchestra under a balmy night sky, usually accompanied by a lightshow and fireworks.

Beaches are never far away from Auckland's suburbs, whether one heads to the east along past Tamaki and the many impressive waterfront residences of Mission Bay, or to the spectacular beaches of the west (where the film *The Piano* was shot) or over the Harbour Bridge to the sprawling North Shore.

Devonport, a maritime suburb with two volcanic cones, one an old Maori pa, has a regular commuter ferry service to downtown Auckland and is charming with many timber villas.

Heading north through the valuable real estate of Takapuna and Milford's wonderful beaches (named the 'Golden Mile') the coastline crawls on through the east coast bays into rural areas.

The Hibiscus Coast beckons with many more stunning views and beaches such as Waiwera and the Wenderholm Regional Park.

The Coromandel Peninsula on the pretty Pacific Coast Highway, only 90 minutes from Auckland, is brimming with Maori and European history and is an artist's haven. At Hot Water Beach on the north-eastern side, you can dig into the sand and sit in a warm sea bath for two hours on either side of the low tide. (Be wary about swimming here.)

Export/Trade Investment Opportunities are specialised software and technology applications, recreational marine, biotechnology, film and television production, tourism and niche marketing. Useful websites are:

www.aucklandnz.com
www.competitive.co.nz
www.innovationharbour.com
www.enterprisens.org.nz
www.aucklandcity.govt.nz
www.enterprisewaitakere.co.nz
www.manukau.govt.nz,
www.innovation.com,
www.investauckland.com
www.aucklandzoo.co.nz
www.thecoromandel.com
www.pacificcoast.co.nz.

The Bay of Plenty has a mild climate that is perfect for growing citrus, kiwi fruit, and avocados. Mount Maunganui, or 'The Mount' as New Zealanders fondly refer to the pristine beach and land in the heart of the Bay of Plenty, was, not so long ago, a place where ramshackle houses and surfers ruled. With a 232-metre extinct volcano at one end and million dollar views it is now home to high-rise apartment blocks and mini-mansions. There is a great holiday atmosphere with cafés, bars and shops and wonderful hot saltwater pools to relax in. Activities like sea kayaking, white water rafting, scuba-diving, fishing and windsurfing abound and for the fearless there is also skydiving or jet boating. A two and a half hour drive from Auckland, the Mount is just a stroll from Tauranga, destined to be New Zealand's fourth biggest city. Two marinas with many charter boats testify to the big game fishing opportunities available. The 'Round the World Alone' yacht race organisers chose the Port of Tauranga for their New Zealand stopover in 2003.

The Bay of Plenty boasts 2,400 hours of sunshine per year and a strong business framework. Planned are a NZ$500 million road network, a 200-hectare business park, a hotel/conference complex, new shopping centres and apartment blocks accompanied by scenery and beaches that are world class Priority One. The region's economic arm is backed by 200 businesses and local councils with the aim of creating 2,500 new jobs through the establishment of approximately 40 new companies over the next five years. Priority One helps business newcomers to the region deal with local authorities and red tape. Leases and rentals are currently very affordable with an over supply of office space in the prime central business district for only approximately NZ$120–NZ$165 per square metre.

New enterprises to date include the Blokart, a cross between a go-kart and a small land yacht, Del Costa Palms, a business that exports mature palms to China, the world renowned Comvita Company with its honey health products and the ride-on lawnmowers made by Trimax. Other industries are slat bed and bedroom furniture manufacture, darts and dartboard manufacture, a telephone tracking system, lily bulb breeding, pet-food manufacture and fruit ingredient products.

Start-up companies range from bio-pharmaceuticals and genetics to natural product extraction, wood processing, equipment manufacture and the growing of exotic Asian vegetables and herbs for export and edible fungi for the home market. There are approximately 8,300 businesses and more than 35,000 full-time employees in the western Bay region. The construction industry accounts for about 10% of the full-time workforce, manufacturing 17%, metal fabrication, machinery and equipment 30%, and food and beverages, 24%.

The Port of Tauranga, the largest round-the-clock export port in the country, is used by 170 exporters. This thriving port, built on a natural harbour and now New Zealand's largest export gateway, flourishes with successful contracts arising from the timber, paper, horticultural and dairy products of the region. The kiwi fruit and avocado sectors are key employers, as are boat-building, marine services, fisheries, aqua-culture and food processing. Zespri International, one of New Zealand's largest exporters, moved its headquarters from Auckland to Tauranga to be close to the kiwi fruit grower customers, who represent 78% of the country's export production. New Zealand produces approximately 65 million trays of kiwi fruit annually. The fourth largest electricity gen-

erator and retailer, Trust Power, and fertiliser manufac-
turers, Balance Agri-Nutrients are also based in
Tauranga.

New homes in a NZ$20 million prime downtown housing
complex were snapped up in May 2003 before being built
and without any advertising. Contact www.priorityone.-
co.nz for more information.

Tauranga means 'anchorage' or 'deep resting place' and
the whole area has huge historical significance as one of
the first canoes, Arawa, with early Maori migrants from
Hawaiki, landed at Maketu. Further south of Tauranga,
Te Puke has four safe beaches and is a popular spot for
surfcasters. Here, or from Whatakane just around the
coast, you can take a boat to experience the great belly
belches of ash and steam from New Zealand's most active
volcano, White Island. Useful websites:

    www.bayofplentynz.com
    www.tauranga.govt.nz
    www.tauranga.co.nz
    www.tauranga.org.nz
    www.mount-manganui.co.nz
    www.tauranga.citynews.co.nz
    www.visitplenty.co.nz
    www.cityoftauranga.co.nz
    www.kiwifruitcountry.co.nz
    www.tepuke.co.nz
    www.whakatane.co.nz
    www.priorityone.co.nz.

The **Hawkes Bay**'s gentle slopes and balmy temperatures

make this region a major fruit grower and home to 34 vineyards, all producers of world-renowned fine wines. At the heart of the bay are the often-overlooked cities of Napier, Havelock North and Hastings, some of the best holiday destinations in the country.

Napier, devastated by an earthquake in 1931 with the loss of 258 lives, rebuilt itself into what is one of the most concentrated collections of Art Deco, Spanish Mission and Stripped Classical buildings in the world today. The region offers constant entertainment and things to do, with festivals of all types including gourmet food of the region, regular wine tastings at the vineyards, vintage car rallies, arts and crafts trails, and the Hawke's Bay Food Group Farmers Market held in the Hastings Showgrounds every Sunday morning. Every year a stunning concert featuring international artists, which has included Dame Kiri Te Kanawa and Spanish singer Julio Iglesias, is held in the natural and very beautiful amphitheatre of the Mission Vineyard.

The gannet colony at Cape Kidnappers, the National Aquarium of New Zealand and the Marineland marine zoo are all worth visiting. Further north is Gisborne, another area rich in Maori history, tradition and culture, where communities with their traditional maraes can be found all down the Pacific Coast Highway on the eastern side. Just north of Gisborne, is Whangara, where the haunting and much acclaimed recent film *Whale Rider* was filmed. Websites:
    www.hawkesbaynz.com
    www.artdeconapier.com

www.gisbornenz.com.

Rotorua (population 56,900) is the thermal heartland of the volcanic centre of the North Island and sits on the shores of Lake Rotorua, one of 16 in the region. Built on top of a steaming underground cauldron caused by a break in the Indo-Pacific and Australasian plates, huge geysers like the awesome Whakarewarewa, angrily spurt forth steaming water, while boiling mud plops away. Locals joke about the sulphuric smells and live alongside steaming vents on front lawns (which are useful for cooking on). Rotorua where the Te Arawa tribe settled 600 years ago and the spiritual home of Maori is visited by more than a million tourists a year, all wanting to experience the many activities and view the essentials of Maori culture. These include the traditional earth-oven hangi meals, Maori concert parties with the menacing-looking haka, the fine artefacts in the museum, the working Arts and Crafts Institute and the thermal village where Maori live and work. Other attractions in Rotorua are the Blue Baths and the Polynesian Spa. Tame trout can be seen in the Paradise Valley Springs and there are many lakes and rivers where brown or rainbow trout are caught. For the more adventurous, there are gondola, boat and luge rides, volcanic flights, white-water rafting and bungee jumping.

As home to the southern hemisphere's largest *pinus radiata* forest plantation, which produces 60% of New Zealand's wood harvest and as one of New Zealand's tourist gems, the Rotorua region provides many unique and varied investment options in tourism, forestry and their associated industries.

Rotorua has earned an international reputation as the country's foremost centre of forestry research. The Centre of Excellence (the Radi Centre offering diploma and degree-level training in wood processing), the Waiariki Institute of Technology, a major supplier of solutions in all aspects of the industry and the Forest Research Institute (a Crown Research Institute) which specialises in forestry development and bio materials are all located here. Science and technology, manufacturing, health and professional services feature alongside clusters of educational facilities that have attracted foreign students to the area. The highly developed transport infrastructure that links roads to a deep-water port is invaluable for industry and enhances the world-class environment and growing tourism industry of accommodation, retail and attraction-based activities. Ideally placed to host events of any size, a planned upgrade of the Rotorua Airport will enhance the attractiveness of the region for tourists. The District Council's business development unit works closely with all businesses both new and existing to maximise their potential. For further information email Rotorua's economic and business development manager Mark Rawson at mark.rawson@rdc.govt.nz. Websites:
    www.rotorua-business.com
    www.rotoruanz.com.

Tourism websites:
    www.rotoruanz.com
    www.whakarewarewa.com
    www.hellsgaterotorua.co.nz

www.okawabay.co.nz.

The lush region of **Waikato** (population 236,200) is just a 90-minute drive south of Auckland, the home of New Zealand's thoroughbred horse breeding industry, the country's dairy capital and, indicative of the affluent lifestyle, has 38 golf courses. The largest agricultural exposition in the Southern Hemisphere, Fieldays, is held each year in June at Mystery Creek. Travelling south through Ngaruawahia, just before Hamilton, can be seen the magnificent Turangawaewae Marae belonging to Queen of the Maori King Movement and also head of the large Tainui Tribal Confederation, Te Arikinui Dame Te Atairangikaahu CBE. Bisected by the Waikato River, New Zealand's largest inland city, Hamilton is on the main train trunk line, has plenty of sporting activity and is home of the Waikato University. Surfers flock to Raglan on the river's western side.

There are tourist activities ranging from hot springs at Waingaro, Te Aroha, Matamata and Kawhia, the kiwi house and bird sanctuary at Otorohanga, hot air ballooning, horse trekking, trail biking and wine tasting. Below ground is Waitomo, a 50km labyrinth of limestone caves and grottoes. Underground streams allow visitors to view the glow-worms in their stunning environment and have created a huge international tourist attraction. Websites:

www.waikatonz.co.nz
www.waitomo.co.nz
www.waitomocaves.co.nz
www.hamiltoncity.co.nz.

Taranaki, on the west coast of the central North island and dominated by the imposing extinct volcano of the same name, has 50 prized surfing areas and is reached by Surf Highway 45. The unique scenery of this region is the setting for Tom Cruise and Billy Connelly's film, *The Last Samurai*.

The area is known for the internationally famous Rhododendron Festival (late October to early November) when the 360-hectare Pukeiti garden becomes a riot of colour as 10,000 blooms burst into life, the excellent Govett-Brewster Art Gallery and for having more artists per head of population than any other region. Belying the turbulent history of the region and the tragedy of the peace-loving people of Parihaka, Taranaki today, is serene with fertile lands and a temperate climate, which contributes to a buoyant economy built on dairying and extensive cropping. The area has instigated sophisticated infrastructure industries, has an oil and petroleum industry that contributes more than NZ$2 billion to the nation's economy and supplies 20% of New Zealand's milk.

Puke Ariki, 'Hill of Chiefs' the unique, integrated museum, information centre and library complex is the largest cultural project in the region, a result of 10 years' planning. It utilises and links all eras from ancient artefacts to the website to provide information and is available on www.pukeariki.com.

South Taranaki is also an important contributor to the national economy and produces 5% of the country's gross domestic product while only having 0.7% of the population. The area is home to the world's largest dairy factory, the Kapuni and Kupe gas sites and the Moanui and Swift petrol production stations, yet is still basically rural. Websites:

www.taranakinz.org
www.newplymouthnz.com
www.kaytiaki.co.nz
www.stdc.co.nz (South Taranaki District Council).

Taupo is an area of lakeside resorts, thermal pools and five challenging golf courses with Wairaki the most elegant and favoured. Peaceful Lake Taupo is a water-logged volcano and an angler's heaven. The largest lake in the country, at 619sq km, it is full of brown and rainbow trout, nice and fat on an abundant supply of freshwater crayfish. Tongariro National Park, a World Heritage site, is comprised of the volcanic trio of Ruapehu, Tongariro and Ngauruhoe, and in summer is a bush-walkers heaven and in winter a major ski resort. Websites:

www.laketauponz.co
www.taupo.com
www.newzealandfishing.com
www.mruapehu.com
www.ruapehunz.com.

The following River Region has the Whanganui, Rangitikei and Manawatu rivers flowing through it. **Manawatu** embraces the student and research-based city of Palmerston North with Massey University, the polytechnic and other centres of learning. Ohakea Air Base and the Linton and Waioru army camps give a military feel to the area.

The area is renowned for beautiful gardens, golf and fishing. The **Wairapapa** is famous for excellent Pinot Noir wines and in November each year celebrates fine food and wines in Toast Martinborough. The country's top sheep shearers compete annually for the Golden Shears Trophy in this quiet long-established sheep-farming region.

Horowhenua is an important beef, dairy, horticultural and floricultural area of New Zealand. Organic food cultivation is increasing rapidly and there are 20 textile companies resident in the region as well. Websites:
www.wairapanz.com
www.pncc.govt.nz
www.armymuseum.co.nz
www.wanganui.org.nz
www.rivernz.com
www.mdc.govt.nz
www.manawatunz.co.nz
www.horowhenua.org.nz
www.enterprisehorowhenua.co.nz.

Wellington (population 415,700) lies on a fault line – the harbour was created by ancient flooding of a huge valley. In 1460, an earthquake pushed up the Miramar Peninsula and the original area of the city had very little flat land. In 1852, reclamation of the land the around the waterfront named Lambton Quay was started and still continues today. In 1855, an earthquake razed part of the Hutt Road and the area from Te Aro out to the Basin Reserve making it flat. Founded on hasty and illegal buying by the New Zealand Company from Maori, who denied they had sold Port Nicholson, or Poneke as they called it, old land rights struggles still plague the area.

The country's seat of political power has a sophisticated café society with over 400 restaurants, many of which are regarded amongst the best in New Zealand.

New Zealand's renowned author Katherine Mansfield was born in Wellington and her childhood home can be found in Tinakori Road.

As the centre for visual and performing arts, the home of the New Zealand Symphony Orchestra and The Royal New Zealand Ballet, Wellington hosts a three-week international arts festival every two years that is full of cultural and literary events. Te Papa, The Museum of New Zealand, The Botanical Gardens, a ride on the cable-car and the refurbished Parliament buildings are all tourist draws. Wellington also has good swimming beaches like Oriental Bay and other places for day trips, such as Days Bay and Matiu-Somes Island, both of which can be reached by a short ferry trip across the harbour. The last 10 years have seen a dynamic marketing input, which has turned the capital into the thriving and prosperous centre of New Zealand. The suburbs crawl northwards past the Hutt Valley and along the Kapiti Coast, currently in hot demand by those wanting property with a sea view.

Export trade investment opportunities are e-business, customer contact centres, software, earthquake engineering, film and television, education optics and tourism. Business contact websites:

www.smartwellington.co.nz
www.upperhutt.org.nz
www.businessporrirua.co.nz
www.huttcity.govt.nz.

Leisure and information websites:
www.wellingtonnz.com
www.wellington.net.nz.

SOUTH ISLAND

Marlborough (population 40,200), just a ferry ride across
the harbour from Wellington, is a centre for whale-
watching, dolphin and seal swimming and eating fresh
crayfish. Queen Charlotte Track is becoming increasingly
popular with walkers for the stunning scenery and
kayakers are well catered for in the region. Boaties flock
to this very peaceful waterway for diving and the stunning
scenery.

The best Sauvignon Blancs in the world are made here in
Blenheim, the heart of Marlborough wine country, and
the biggest wine producers in New Zealand. More than 50
wineries offer tastings and there are also cottage
industries selling olive oil and preserves. Websites:
www.blenheim.co.nz
www.whalewatch.co.nz
www.kaikoura.co.nz
www.dolphin.co.nz
www.marlboroughsounds.co.nz.

Nelson, (population 82,100), named after the man who
won the Battle of Trafalgar, is one of the top destinations

for South Islanders' summer holidays and visitors looking for good beaches and some of the finest national parks in the country – Kahurangi, the well known Abel Tasman and the Nelson Lakes National Park. Also home to the high profile, original and creative annual Montana New Zealand Wearable Art Awards. In February, crowds flock to the Taste Nelson Festival for wonderful seafood. The regional cuisine is beautifully presented at the many stylish waterfront cafés.

There are plenty of adrenaline sports like tandem parachute jumps, kayaking, mountain biking and skiing. Export and trade investment activities are wine, vine-yards, tourism, horticulture, forestry, seafood and art.

Business website:
www.ncc.govt.nz.

Leisure and information websites:
www.nelsonnz.com
www.abeltasman.co.nz
www.skydive.co.nz.

West Coast and Fiordland (population 22,000) is an area which covers five of New Zealand's 13 National Parks. In recognition of their pristine state they have been declared World Heritage Sites by the United Nations. This thin strip of land with the Tasman Sea on one side and the majestic Southern Alps on the other is a major source of greenstone, and is renowned for the stunning walking tracks that entice hikers from all over the world. The Heaphy and Milford tracks are full of native birds and the mysterious and awesome Fox and Franz Josef Glaciers are memorable. The region is known for its annual zany Wild Foods Festival, boutique beer brewers, dairying and logging. Fishing, hunting and lake cruising to exclusive lodges are other tourist activities.

Export and trade investment opportunities are tourism, mining, horticultural, seafood, forestry and food.

Business websites:
    www.greymouthnz.co.nz
    www.bullerdc.govt.nz

Leisure websites:
    www.westcoast.org.nz
    www.west-coast.co.nz
    www.hokitika.com
    www.westport.org.nz
    www.rivers.co.nz.

Canterbury (population 473,300), with the biggest city in the South Island, Christchurch, is one of the flattest and driest areas of New Zealand. Christchurch, a picturesque and neat city with restored neo-Gothic buildings and churches and the meandering Avon River, reflects a British heritage. The International Antarctic Centre, dozens of art and craft galleries and Orana Wildlife Reserve are tourist draws as are the sporting activities like skiing, golfing, fishing, ballooning, skydiving and river rafting. Hanmer Springs, the outdoor hot mineral baths and Arthur's Pass, an alpine retreat with fishing, hiking and jet boating are also popular.

Ashburton and Timaru are close to rivers and surf and have created new industry because of the entrepreneurial spirit of enthusiastic locals. Further south is **Geraldine** with massive hydroelectric dams and lakes offering an adventurer's paradise of mountain biking, rock climbing, white water rafting, skiing and fishing.

Export and trade opportunities in the area are research and development organisation, software development, biotechnology, high technology manufacturing, tourism and education. Websites:

www.christchurch.org.nz

www.christchurchnz.net

www.canterburypages.co.nz

www.cae.canterbury.ac.nz

www.whatsoninchristchurch.co.nz

www.ccc.govt.nz

www.ashburton.co.nz

www.hurunui.co.nz

www.cdc.org.nz.

Otago (population 187,200) is home to a colony of royal albatrosses, little yellow-eyed and blue penguins and large populations of fur seals and sea lions on Tairoa Head located on the Otago Peninsula. Scottish Presbyterian immigrants, who landed at the harbour entrance of Port Charmers in 1848, founded Dunedin, which in Gaelic means Edinburgh. By that time, after disease introduced to Maori by sealers and whalers, and inter-tribal feuding, the considerable population of the Otakau Pa was reduced to just 100.

The city was built on the wealth of the 1860's gold rush and is full of magnificent Victorian and Edwardian stately homes and buildings, with a railway station proclaimed to be the grandest in the southern hemisphere. The county's oldest university is located here, out of which a thriving biotech industry has grown. Author Janet Frame and playwright Roger Hall were born here and many of New Zealand's fashion designers started their career in the creative environment that has attracted artisans and musicians.

Speights the beer brewers and Cadbury's chocolate factory are both well-established industries. **Central Otago**, a heritage and very pretty area, is the fastest growing winemaking region in New Zealand. There are many cafés, which are perfect for sipping a Pinot Gris or Chardonnay. Alexandra and Cromwell sustain a thriving stone-fruit industry and the flooded Clutha River, which provides the hydro source for the Clyde Dam, is a watersports haven. Export and trade opportunities are research and development organisations, software development, biotechnology, high technology, manufacturing, tourism and education. Websites:
www.cityofdunedin.com
www.visit-dunedin.co.nz.

Queenstown (population 7,500) creates a memorable welcome, with the Remarkables vertical peaks a breath away as you bank steeply and fly over Lake Whakatipu, above the Kawerau and Shotover Rivers and gaze out at the spectacular snow covered Coronet Peak.

Born in 1860 amidst the gold rush and named after Queen Victoria, Queenstown offers every sport that one could want to indulge in. Heli skiing, parapenting, bungee-jumping (the home of), and trout fishing are only a few of the activities available in this self-styled 'adventure capital' of the world. This formerly sleepy hollow now boasts excellent skiing facilities, world class grapes, wonderful restaurants, designer golf courses and luxurious lodgings. Websites:

www.queenstown-nz.co.nz
www.AJHackett.com
www.bungy.co.nz
www.grandcanyon.co.nz
www.skyalpine.co.nz
www.shotoverjet.com
www.millbrook.co.nz
www.arrowtown.com
www.winecentral.co.nz.

Southland is renowned for the fat bluff oysters obtainable from the most southern tip of the South Island and sold all around New Zealand when in season. **Invercargill**, (population 50,000) is similar to Dunedin with a strong Scottish ancestry and stately Victorian and Edwardian buildings.

The wealth of this region began when milk prices soared and farmers came from all over to run their dairy herds on the rich green pastures. Locals are promoting the area as a place to do business and receive education.

The region is only beginning to enjoy a tourist industry as

it has just started to actively market the rugged vistas and dense forests of rimu, kamiai and silver beech laced with the rivers and waterfalls of Fiordland. A new three-day walk along the Humpridge Track is attracting hikers eager to experience the vast array of birds and wildlife. Wetlands and tiny offshore islands provide sanctuary to threatened native bird species. Stewart Island, New Zealand's third biggest island is just a short boat ride from Bluff and is a remote wildlife haven. Websites:

    www.envirosouth.govt.nz

    www.southland.org.nz

    www.southland.nz.com

    www.venturesouthland.co.nz.

13

Housing

New Zealand has a high level of home ownership and, for many English immigrants, the best thing about living in New Zealand is the unrestricted choice of house, especially if you want to build. The important thing to remember about living down under is that the sun comes from the north so a priority is a northerly aspect, particularly in the living areas. To climb into a bed warmed by sunshine is a delight so northerly facing bedrooms are desirable, but not as important as the general aspect.

Buying and renting in Auckland and her suburbs is the most expensive with Wellington close behind. Initially, renting is probably the best option. Generally, there is a demand for rental properties with a wide variation in prices and quality.

Decide if you want to be close to schools, shops and public transport, how far you want to travel to work and what sort of neighbourhood you prefer. Ideal for individuals or young couples, apartments are a relatively new way of living for New Zealanders. They offer convenient inner city living but may be small compared to suburban properties and lack a garden. If you choose to be close to the water, remember that rentals with a sea view or a beach within walking distance command a premium rental.

Most properties are usually timber or brick and tile, and will have a garage or plenty of parking space. If you find a property you like, you will need to make a quick decision as the demand for reasonable rental dwellings is currently high.

Most rental properties are unfurnished, but will have a fridge, oven, curtains, carpets and usually laundry facilities (washing machine) and maybe a dishwasher (whiteware)

Many parts of New Zealand can be cold, especially in winter, so you will have to provide your own heaters. Dampness and mould can be a problem in winter if the house is not aired and has little sun.

FINDING A RENTAL PROPERTY

Real estate agencies are a good place to start but the desirable properties go quickly, so get to know the letting agent who will call you as soon as a good property comes in. Letting centres usually have a 'hook' of a very desirable property to arouse your interest and will charge you to join them and use their services. National and local newspaper 'To let' columns on Saturdays and Wednesdays are another option but, again, you need to start early and phone as soon as you see the advertisement. New Zealand has very solid legislation which protects both tenants and landlords. At this stage it is a good idea to contact Tenancy Services (www.tenancy.govt.nz) who will advise you of your rights as a tenant and what is expected of you, the tenant.

Understanding real estate advertisements

Advertisements for both rental and purchase of property use the following abbreviations:

Ac	–	air conditioning
ono	–	or nearest offer
alc	–	alcove
ophws	–	off-peak hot-water system
BEO	–	Buyer Enquiry Offer
osp	–	off-street parking
Bi	–	built-in
oyo	–	own your own
Bics	–	built-in cupboards
pa	–	per annum
Biw	–	built-in wardrobe
pmth	–	per month
Bt	–	brick walls with a tile roof floor
psn	–	position
CBD	–	Central Business District
Pol flr	–	polished floor
Bv	–	brick with veneer
pwk	–	per week
Cpds	–	cupboards
QV	–	Quotable Valuation
Ctl	–	cement tile
rc	–	reverse cycle

CV	–	Commercial Value
rend	–	rendered
Det	–	detached
rf	–	roof
Elf	–	electric light fittings
row	–	right of way
Elhws	–	electric hot-water service
RV	–	rateable value
Ens	–	en suite bathroom
sb	–	solid brick
Fib	–	fibro cement
sep din	–	separate dining room
Fitts	–	fittings
sep/shwr	–	separate shower
Fl covs	–	floor coverings
Shwr rcs	–	shower recess
F/furn	–	fully furnished
s'out	–	sleepout
F tld	–	fully tiled
stca	–	subject to council approval
Ghws	–	gas hot water service
tc	–	tile
GV	–	Government Valuation
tf	–	timberframe
Ingr pl	–	inground pool
Tld rf	–	tiled roof
K'ette	–	kitchenette
umr	–	under main roof
Ldr	–	lounge dining room
Ven blds	–	venetian blinds
L'fitt	–	light fittings
ver	–	verandah

Lug	–	lockup garage
vp	–	vacant possession
LV	–	Land Value
wb	–	weather board
Neg	–	negotiable
wi	–	wrought iron
Ofp	–	open fireplace
wi pant	–	walk-in pantry
oil/htr	–	oil heater
ww crpt	–	wall-to-wall carpet

Being a tenant

The main tenancies are:

1. *Periodic tenancies* are tenancies without a fixed time of tenancy. Usually ended by either party giving a pre-arranged period of notice that by law is usually either 42 or 90 days for landlords, and 21 days for tenants. Most tenancies are like this.

2. *Fixed-term tenancies* are where the fixed date cannot be changed. Fixed-term tenancies not fully covered by the residential Tenancies Act 1986 are tenancies of less than 120 days, or are of five years or more or an agreement that stipulates it operates outside of the Act. Again contact Tenancy Services before signing any contract.

Below is a list of the approximate average rental price for 2002 for a standard, unfurnished three-bedroom house in NZ dollars. Rentals have increased since this list was compiled and approximately another NZ$80–$100 could be added to the figures below. Please note this is a guide only and you will need to clarify rentals in the area that you choose to live in.

Standard three bedroom unfurnished house.

Location	Per week (NZ$)
Auckland Central	438.00
Auckland North	242.00
Auckland South	267.00
Auckland West	276.00
Wellington Lower Hutt	342.00
Wellington Upper Hutt	230.00
Wellington Mt Victoria	410.00
Nelson Central	248.00
West Coast Buller	108.00
Christchurch Riccarton	247.00
Christchurch Central	231.00
Christchurch Papanui	253.00
Dunedin Mosgiel	168.00
Dunedin St Clair	181.00
Queenstown	287.00
Invercargill	160.00
Southland District	110.00

If you find a property through a letting agent they will charge you a commission of *one week's rent* once the rental contract is complete.

A bond will also have to be paid that amounts to *two to four weeks' rental*. The landlord will provide you with a Bond Lodgement Form that both you and the landlord have to sign. The landlord must then deposit the original form and your accompanying cheque with the Tenancy

Services Centre within 23 working days of receiving it. A receipt is then sent to you and the landlord.

The landlord will also provide you with a Tenancy Agreement Form in plain language which sets out the conditions of the lease. You both need to agree on details, sign and each keep a copy. Also, as part of the above form, there is a Property Inspection Report where you and the landlord together record and check the condition of the chattels, furniture, fittings and exterior. Carefully go through the different sections and if anything is amiss like a mark on the carpet, make sure it is recorded to both of your satisfactions and initialled. You both have a copy to keep and when you leave it is a record of the condition of everything that cannot be disputed.

When you hand in your notice to leave, the landlord will inspect the property. If the property is in the same condition as you found it, less general wear and tear, and your rent is paid up to date you will be refunded the bond in full. If, for example the carpet is damaged, quotes will be obtained and the bond used to pay the final bill. So it is in your best interests to look after the rental property as you would your own.

To recover your bond, complete a Bond Refund Form, and ensure both you and your landlord sign it and send it to Tenancy Services. If there is any disagreement over the bond, contact Tenancy Services.

Approximate payments when you rent a property:

Rental of NZ$300 per week
Four weeks rent as a bond NZ$1200
Rent (usually paid two weekly in advance) NZ$600
One week's rent as commission to the agent NZ$375
(NZ$300+ GST of 12.5%)
Total NZ$2175.00

You will also need to pay for the connection of services like electricity, gas, and telephone, which could be approximately NZ$300. The local council bills you quarterly for the water usage, and rates include rubbish collection (plus NZ$1.00 for every bag you put out as a recycling incentive).

Tenancy agreements must include:

♦ names and addresses of the landlord and tenant
♦ permanent addresses for service of both the above and the property address
♦ date the agreement is signed
♦ date the tenancy starts
♦ bond amount
♦ rent amount and how often it is to be paid
♦ place or bank account number where the rent is to be paid
♦ any agent or legal fees paid
♦ a list of chattels.

Ending a tenancy requires 21 days' signed notice in writing. A landlord must give a tenant 90 days' notice (or 42 days in some circumstances) in writing and both parties are required to add an extra four working days if the notice is sent by post.

Tenants must:

- pay the rent on time
- use the property as a home
- keep the property clean and tidy
- repair any damage they or their guests have caused
- permit no more than the specified number of residents
- depart on or before the final day of tenancy
- remove all goods and rubbish and ensure the property is tidy and clean
- return all keys
- leave all the chattels in good order
- provide access to prospective tenants or buyers
- only use the property for legal purposes
- pay all agreed and outstanding charges.

Must not:
- alter the property or change the locks
- refuse rightful entry to the landlord or an authorised agent
- sublet or transfer the tenancy.

Landlords' responsibilities:
- If a landlord wants to increase the rent, 60 days' notice must be given in writing but it must not be within six months of the start of the tenancy or the previous increase.
- They must give 48 hours' notice of an inspection and 24 hours' notice of entry for repairs.
- Inform the tenant of plans to sell the property.

- Ensure locks and catches are secure.
- Provide receipts for all payments.
- Provide rent statements if requested.
- Do necessary repairs and pay for urgent ones.
- Present a clean and habitable property.
- Pay costs of property insurance and rates.
- Ensure that tenants are not disturbed unnecessarily.
- Landlords by law are not allowed to discriminate against anyone for reasons of race, sex, colour, ethnic origin, disability or religious beliefs. Contact the Human Rights Commission if you feel you have been discriminated against at www.hrc.co.nz.

The landlord (and this is one of the benefits of renting) usually undertakes repairs. If you are unable to contact the landlord or he is taking a while to get the job done you can send him or her a letter requesting that the work be done within ten working days. If it is urgent, have the work done and the landlord must reimburse you. If in doubt or there are any problems, contact Tenancy Services first. They may refer you to the Tenancy Tribunal, an independent body for mediation or resolving disputes. The landlord will have insurance to cover the building, but the tenant will require contents insurance to cover their belongings.

To download the Tenancy Lodgement, Tenancy Agreements, Property Inspection Report and Bond Refund forms, visit: www.tenancy.govt.nz. Forms can also be purchased from major stationery stores like Whitcoulls and Warehouse Stationery outlets.

www.tenancy.govt.nz also provides free advice on all

aspects of renting.

BUYING A HOME

Most New Zealanders' goal is to own their piece of land and they usually achieve this. Buying a house in New Zealand is a relatively uncomplicated and speedy process that takes place in a well-legislated environment, which protects both the vendor and buyer.

The range of properties to choose from is enormous and for those seeking the lifestyle of their dreams, it is quite possible that they will find it. City housing ranges from modern apartment blocks to recently refurbished buildings that have been converted into apartments, to delightful wooden villas, many recently restored, to modern shapes of glass and concrete that embrace the New Zealand lifestyle. Very popular are lifestyle rural blocks with custom-built homes on ten acres or more.

Houses are mainly stand alone, have plenty of privacy, lots of room and often cach is as different from its neighbour as possible. Gardens, barbeque areas and swimming pools abound and some lucky people have riparian rights with their yacht moored at the bottom of their garden. Otherwise the boat may be in the middle of construction on the front lawn! Houses are usually set back well away from the road and the separate letterbox is at the front gate.

Building materials vary and although most homes are insulated, they don't usually have double-glazing or central heating. Open fires, wood burners, gas and electricity are the main forms of heating.

Prices vary depending on the area, with Auckland city more expensive than Wellington. Find out as much as possible about an area before you buy. Is it close to schools, shops, and public transport? Is it a reasonable distance to travel to work, as the peak times can be very congested?

Check out the following website for price comparisons as values have increased dramatically in the last few years: www.quotable.co.nz.

Do not be pressured by real estate agents who are very keen to make a sale. The market can be very competitive which means you will usually be well looked after if you are a genuine buyer. Ask to see prices of recent properties for sale in the area you have chosen. Study the papers, especially the property sections on Wednesday and Saturday or the Classified Advertisements, www.nzherald.co.nz/property, www.propertystuff.co.nz and real estate agents' windows. There are also plenty of free publications available to guide you. National listings are available through The Real Estate Institute that also provides an up-to-date survey of mortgage interest rates and access to a handy mortgage calculator on www.realenz.co.nz.

Although it is not a legal requirement, many house buyers prefer to employ a lawyer to assist with their purchase. A lawyer will guide you through the sales process and protect your interests. Their services generally include:

- helping you to negotiate the purchase and price with the owners
- a 'title search' to make sure that there are no legal problems
- checking the contract
- advising you if there are any factors like tax that may affect you
- drawing up the documents to transfer ownership
- arranging the settlement
- letting you know your rights.

Conveyancers who specialise in private sales and real estate agents also provide these services.

Real estate agents work on commission and sell most of the properties. Depending on their qualifications, their commission is a portion of the 1–3% fee, which is negotiated by their office and paid by the vendor. The balance goes towards maintaining the office, overheads and advertising costs. Although the agent is in effect paid by a vendor when he sells their realty, he will make appointments to take you out to see other properties. You don't have to stay with only one agent as some agents will know of houses that are about to come on the market and you may be the lucky first viewer. Other agents will have listings to themselves and no matter who sells the property he will receive a percentage (this doesn't affect you). If you purchase a property that another agent showed you at an earlier date he or she is entitled to the commission.

Real estate agents in New Zealand
L. J. Hooker (NZ) – www.ljhooker.co.nz. Property

management specialists, providing searchable listings
of residential, rental, rural and vacant land properties.

RealEnz – www.realenz.co.nz. Official property directory
of the Real Estate Institute of New Zealand. Features
a property search, buying and selling information, and
finance calculators.

Real Estate Institute of New Zealand (REINZ) –
www.reinz.org.nz. Property news and statistics, arti-
cles, books and up-coming events.

Bayleys Real Estate – www.bayleys.co.nz. Realtors in New
Zealand with real estate and industrial property for
sale as well as waterfront and residential investment
property.

Harcourts Real Estate – www.harcourts.co.nz. Offers a
wide range of resources from more than 145 offices
and over 1,200 real estate consultants nationwide.

Property Council of New Zealand – www.propertynz.
co.nz. Core business activities: advocacy, networking,
information, and communication.

Ray White Real Estate – www.RayWhite.net. Australian,
New Zealand and South East Asian property network
with over 530 offices throughout Australasia.

Property Brokers Ltd – www.propertybrokers.co.nz. Sales
in the Lower North Island. Database of properties
categorised by type and location.

Open2View.com – www.open2view.com. Property listing
service with photographic and 360-degree virtual
tours of various types of properties.

New Zealand Property Index – www.nzpi.co.nz. A
complete guide for buyers, sellers and investors, of
New Zealand residential property with free software
downloads, feature properties, hints and tips to make

sound property decisions.

FlatmatesNZ.com – www.flatmatesnz.com. Helps users find flats and flatmates in New Zealand. Search the database or place a listing free.

Barfoot and Thompson – www.barfoot.co.nz. Features residential, rural and commercial listings in Auckland and surrounding districts as well as company information.

NetHomes – www.nethomes.co.nz. Promotes real estate for sale in New Zealand. Online search facility.

The Professionals – www.The-Professionals.co.nz. Ninety offices across New Zealand. All offices are privately owned and managed by experienced people who live in the area.

NZ Property Resource Centre – www.nzpropertyresource.co.nz. An independent resource for property-related information.

Landlords.co.nz – www.landlords.co.nz. NZ's top Landlord and Property Investors resource. Property investment news, forms, letters, book reviews, users forum and chat.

Valuers net.nz – www.valuers.net.nz. A property consultancy company covering New Zealand.

Rural Real Estate – www.rural-realestate.co.nz. The place to buy and sell rural properties in New Zealand.

Harvey Real Estate Ltd – www.harveys.co.nz. Focused on the North Island, searchable property database.

Free Real Estate – www.freerealestate.co.nz. This site puts property sellers and buyers in touch with each other and provides help for those looking for New Zealand property resources on the web.

New Zealand Commercial Property Brokers Ltd. –

ww.nzcpb.co.nz. Investment properties. Information on New Zealand, immigration, New Zealand investments and property opportunities. Site in English and German languages.

Fletcher Residential Ltd: New Homes – www.newhome. co.nz. New homes for sale listed by region. A subsidiary of Fletcher Challenge.

Flatline.co.nz – www.flatline.co.nz. Provides a source of rental property for all of New Zealand. Free to search and find flats with a minimal fee to landlords for placing advertisements.

Xtra's Real Estate channel page – xtramsn.co.nz.real_estate. Provides nationwide searchable properties for sale or rent. A subsidiary of Telecom NZ.

New Zealand Property Investors Federation – www.nzpif.org.nz A resource for members of the NZPIF and information for property investors interested in joining a federation association.

Propertystuff – www.propertystuff.co.nz. www.real-estate-nz.com is a property guide for migrants and overseas investors focusing on Christchurch.

Property values in New Zealand are increasing. The national median in residential prices rose from NZ$227,000 in October 2003 to NZ$235,000 in November 2003. As the Auckland market is easing, the Wellington market is driving prices up. According to REINZ, this trend is caused by recent interest rate increases, immigration and a housing shortage in some areas. (See Figure 12 for price comparisons.)

Open homes are usually held on a Saturday for two hours

Property Market Report
Total dwellings median price comparisons for
November 1996–2003

Region	Nov 00 NZ$	Nov 01 NZ$	Nov 02 NZ$	Oct 03 NZ$	Nov 03 NZ$
Northland	159,000	154,000	157,750	185,000	176,500
Auckland	240,000	245,000	280,000	325,770	320,000
Waikato/BOP/Gisborne	158,000	163,250	169,000	186,500	189,500
Hawkes Bay	132,000	135,000	140,000	172,750	180,000
Manawatu/Wanganui	108,000	108,000	111,000	116,750	118,000
Taranaki	106,000	112,500	115,000	134,000	140,500
Wellington	197,000	206,500	222,000	257,000	262,000
Nelson/Marlborough	147,750	151,000	175,500	251,200	261,000
Canterbury/Westland	143,750	140,000	149,950	179,000	180,000
Otago	95,000	100,000	115,500	146,000	155,500
Southland	72,750	80,000	84,375	133,500	115,990

Region	Nov 96 NZ$	Nov 97 NZ$	Nov 98 NZ$	Nov 99 NZ$
Northland	125,000	140,000	145,000	142,000
Auckland	225,000	245,000	227,000	238,050
Waikato/BOP/Gisborne	140,000	152,000	155,000	165,000
Hawkes Bay	120,000	122,750	123,000	127,000
Manawatu/Wanganui	100,000	102,500	101,250	107,000
Taranaki	105,000	100,000	97,500	102,250
Wellington	153,000	161,000	168,000	175,000
Nelson/Marlborough	135,000	131,500	132,500	145,000
Canterbury/Westland	135,000	145,000	140,000	145,000
Otago	100,000	95,000	89,000	95,000
Southland	80,000	87,500	76,000	75,000

Supplied by the Real Estate Institute of New Zealand (REINZ)

Figure 12. Property market price comparisons.

and advertised in the weekly and local papers. They offer a good opportunity to view and get an idea of values in the area without having to rely on the agent.

There is always talk of the Quotable Valuation (QV) when discussing house prices. This is a benchmark figure, which the local authority sets and publishes yearly on the values of land and the building. This figure is influenced by inflation, timing of the valuation and previous sales figures, and is usually used as a guide for the sales price, although the sales figure – depending on the economy – can be more or less. The Government Valuation (GV) is similar but published every three years and generally affects rates. If the GV increases that means rates will also increase and, conversely, if the GV falls the property value is reduced, so the GV will always attract heated discussion or howls of fury. The rateable charges, which the property owner pays for road maintenance, rubbish collection and public services, like parks, swimming pools and libraries, are based on this figure.

ORGANISING A MORTGAGE

The biggest purchase you will make is usually your house and it is dictated by the amount of finance available. If you have cash you are in a very strong position and can often negotiate a price reduction. Most purchasers require a mortgage to buy their home. The exchange rate is favourable for most immigrants and they feel they get value for their money.

The mortgage industry is competitive and you can contact your bank or financial advisor or go directly to a mortgage broker. Processing is very efficient and often a representative will visit you at home to complete the paperwork for your loan, which can be arranged in 24 hours if necessary. Mortgages are available for up to 95% of the property's value depending on your personal circumstances and ability to repay.

The criteria is that 33% of your gross take home pay is the maximum debt repayment allowable and lending institutions generally like to see a 25% deposit. Shop around as there are many different types of finance available. Some loans have variable rates, fixed rates, principal and interest, interest only or revolving credit facilities which is a fixed rate for half of the amount and a floating rate for the balance which can go up or down. This balance can be used like a credit card and if salaries and any other money is paid into it, the mortgage will reduce rapidly. Repayments made fortnightly rather than monthly will reduce the interest more quickly and therefore the amount borrowed.

You will need to provide information on and proof of:

◆ your earnings
◆ your assets (security against the mortgage)
◆ your liabilities
◆ your living costs.

This information is confidential and will not be passed on to other businesses. Fees for arranging finance vary widely and if you have enough clout you may be able to negotiate with your bank or lender to reduce or eliminate the fee. It is usually a percentage of the purchase price or may be a flat rate of NZ$100–NZ$250.

Insurance companies will also be keen to offer you a mortgage. The safest option when buying a house is to have a Conditional Agreement (see page 210) which will give you time to check important details. After you have paid the deposit you need to speak with your conveyancing solicitor, who will arrange a search of council records to make sure that there is no planned road or major construction that could diminish the value of your planned purchase. He will also check the title and the plans to make sure that you are buying what you think you are buying. You will also need to have a valuation of your property done. This is very worthwhile and may identify potential problems. Try www.quotable.co.nz or ask your real estate agent for a registered valuer living locally.

Real estate terms used in New Zealand that may differ from other countries are:

◆ **Agreement** is the written contract for the sale and purchase of the property between the vendor (seller) and the purchaser (buyer).

◆ **Chattels** are movable and removable items, and may include the refrigerator, television aerial, floor coverings, paintings, blinds, curtains, drapes, and light fittings, as well as furniture, garden items and personal effects. Unless chattels are specified in the agreement, which can be a point of negotiation, they are the seller's property and will be taken away. Most homes for sale in New Zealand do include curtains, fixed floorings, light fittings and, by law, a stove.

• **Conditional Agreement** is a legally binding contract which means the property will not be bought or sold until certain conditions of the agreement are fulfilled (like organising finance or selling an existing property by a fixed time) or have taken place, usually by the purchaser. Conditions can also be included by the purchaser requiring the vendor to do something by a specified date, e.g. that settlement will take place when the house has been painted, the patio repaired or rubbish removed. These clauses of the second type protect the purchaser and allow him or her to delay settlement without penalty or to claim damages if the conditions are not met.

• **Unconditional Agreement** is a legal contract that binds both the purchaser and the vendor to settle on the agreed price on the agreed date. It is not subject to any conditions being satisfied. You should only enter into an Unconditional Agreement if you are absolutely sure that this is a property you want to purchase and that you have funds organised and available to pay the full price. Often if the property is desirable there will be pressure to buy, as the agent will tell you of other interested parties, but don't make the commitment unless you are absolutely sure of the above.

• **Deposit** is usually 10% of the purchase price and is paid by the purchaser or homebuyer when the agreement is signed. This deposit is usually unrefundable and a binding gesture of intent on the purchaser's part. Do not pay the deposit unless you are committed and sure that your finances have been arranged to purchase the property. The deposit is held in trust by the real estate agent's office until settlement when the contract becomes unconditional and then paid to the vendor. This payment basically covers the agent's fee and any expenses they may incur. If anything goes wrong the balance is usually paid to the vendor.

◆ **Freehold** is absolute ownership of land and sometimes known as a 'Fee Simple Estate'. Buildings and fixtures on the land generally belong to the owner of the land.

◆ **Leasehold** is occupation of the land under a lease whereby the owner charges a rental on the land and the occupant or lessee obtains the right to occupy the land for a specified term at a specified rent. Any improvements to the land, like buildings or additions, legally belong to the occupant but the ownership will be subject to the terms of the lease. Some parts of Auckland (Kohimarama and St John's) are leasehold land owned by the church. The dilemma is whether it is best to pay a small amount near the end of the lease and risk a steep increase when the lease is due for renewal or to bite the bullet and pay for the security of the longer term.

◆ **Pre-Approved Home Loan Certificate** confirms that a homebuyer is eligible to borrow a specific amount of home finance from a bank. These are usually issued before a buyer starts to look for a property. Different banks will issue these certificates for different periods of up to three months.

* **Title** or **Certificate of Title** confers legal right of ownership of a property and is a very important document. A copy is usually held by the lender (bank) for the duration of the loan and the original/duplicate is held at the local Land Registry Office.

* **Unit Title** is a form of ownership of apartment, flats and home units whereby each owner obtains full freehold ownership of his or her particular dwelling and any attached ancillary units like a garage or parking space. This is clearly defined on the unit plan and referred to as a **stratum estate**. Each owner is usually a member of a corporate body for administration and the handling of any other issues regarding all the units on the particular unit plan.

MAKING AN OFFER

When you find the house you want you need to make a formal offer in writing on a standard contract form that your agent will supply. A lawyer is not essential but it may reassure you to have another opinion before you present your offer to the vendor.

Sometimes there may be counter offers so your initial proposed offer is not certain until it is accepted by the vendor in writing. This can be a time of great anxiety and the agent will run around so it is important to be available. The deposit is paid on acceptance and the lawyer or agent is legally required to hold the deposit for ten working days or until the conditions of sale are met.

Settlement date or the date that the property becomes yours will be on the contract and that is the date that the lawyer pays the full amount and your contract becomes unconditional. Then you can celebrate. Make sure that your insurance commences on the day you take possession of your new house. At an auction the risk may pass directly to the purchaser as the contract is signed.

Useful contacts
www.landonline.govt.nz is the database of land title and survey information available on a user pays basis.

BUILDING YOUR OWN HOUSE
Building a house is a long-term option you may consider once you are settled. This requires careful evaluation of finances, location and design. The following websites will give you somewhere to start:

◆ Architects Education and Registration Board maintains is database of registered architects – www.aerb.org.nz.

◆ Building Research Association of New Zealand Inc establishes and monitors NZ building standards – www.branz.org.nz.

◆ New Zealand Institute of Building Surveyors Inc represents professional building consultants and provides a list of services and affiliated members – www.buildingsurveyors.co.nz.

◆ Insurance Council of New Zealand provides guidance on all aspects of property and insurance matters – www.icnz.org.nz.

- New Zealand Registered Master Builders Federation lists certified master builders and gives useful information about building a home – www.masterbuilder.org.nz.

- New Zealand Institute of Architects is the professional association of architects – www.nzia.co.nz.

Building inspection reports

Building inspections for new homes arc undertaken by local councils. Building inspections for existing homes are completed by private consultants. Land Information Memoranda is provided by local councils and listings are in the telephone book under 'Local Government Services' or visit Local Government New Zealand at www.lgnz.co.nz.

Other useful sites

- New Zealand Property Institute (NZPI) sets the standards for property valuers and maintains a database of affiliated valuers – www.property.org.nz.

- Specialists in private sales – www.propertyweb.co.nz.

- QV Valuations are responsible for the rating valuations in New Zealand – www.quotable.co.nz.

- Royal Institution of Chartered Surveyors (RICS) – www.rics.org.au.

- ValGroup is an association of independent valuing firms – www.valgroup.co.nz.

- Consumer's Institute of New Zealand is an up-to-date consumer's guide to property rentals and purchase which also covers legal rights of landlords and tenants – www.consumer.org.nz.

◆ The UBD Directory is a comprehensive listing of businesses, products and trade suppliers. It also includes a database of rental accommodation, real estate agents and building trades – www.ubd.co.nz.

◆ This specialist site provides comparative cost-of-living data on a worldwide basis – www.directmoving.com.

14 General Living Expenses

FOOD PRICE GUIDE

These are the Statistics New Zealand official average retail prices for basic food items. All prices are in NZ dollars and are per kilo unless stated. Please note these prices are a guide only and will differ from city to city, shop to shop and season to season.

For a family of four, weekly grocery spending would be approximately NZ$170.00 per week. Price indications in NZ dollars are as follows:

	NZ$
Milk (2 litres)	3.19
Butter (500g)	2.30
Margarine (500g)	2.69
Eggs (per 12)	3.70
Cheese (250g)	3.35
Bread (1 loaf)	2.68
Cereal	3.98
Jam (500g)	2.20

	NZ$
Coffee (instant 100g)	3.99
Tea bags (100)	4.15
Flour	1.39
Rice (1kg)	1.80
Sugar (1.5kg)	1.96
Mince (500g)	5.00
Sirloin steak (500g)	8.00
Lamb roast (per kg)	12.49
Chicken drumsticks (6)	5.50
Chicken breasts (500g)	10.00
Mushrooms (250g)	3.00
Tomatoes (1kg)	4.50
Frozen peas (1kg)	2.00
Oranges (1kg)	1.50
Apples (1kg)	1.70
Bananas (1kg)	2.80
Potatoes (1kg)	1.65
Carrots (1kg)	1.49
Toilet paper (4 rolls)	3.02
Dishwashing liquid	1.98
Washing powder	3.49
Deodorant	3.50
Shampoo	4.99
Toothpaste	2.20
Soap (one)	0.70
Cigarettes (per pack of 25)	10.70

NON-GROCERY COSTS

Levi jeans	99.00
Nike Cross trainers	99–169.00
Movie tickets (per person)	11.00

	NZ$
Video rental	6.00
Normal postage (per letter)	0.40
Car rental (per day)	65–85.00
Bottle of wine	20.00
1 lager beer at bar (333ml)	5.00
1 cappucino	3.00
Colour film 24/400	9.89
Haircuts	15–50.00
Baby-sitting (per hour)	10.00
Golf – green fees (country course)	20.00
Chinese restaurant family dinner for four	60.00
Pizza (large) delivered to home	20.00
Newspaper	1.00
Taxi fare (per km)	1.80

HEALTH COSTS

Doctor (GP) visits: Adult	35–45
6–17 year olds	20.00
Children under 6	Free

(Weekend and evening appointments
may cost NZ$5–NZ$10 extra)

Subsidised medicine prescriptions:	
Adult (maximum)	15.00
Children (maximum)	10.00
Dental check-up	50.00
Private health insurance (per year)	350–3,800

PET EXPENSES

Vet consultation	32.00
Cat food (385g tin)	1.44

	NZ$
Dog food (2kg dry)	4.56

BANKING COSTS

	NZ$
Monthly fees	3.00
Each manual transaction	0.50–1.00
Electronic transaction	0.25–0.50
Telephone banking	0.25–0.50

HOMEWARE COSTS

Guide to the costs of purchasing furniture, whiteware and other products for the home.

	Medium quality NZ$	Excellent quality NZ$
Refrigerator	350–1,000	5,800 +
Washing machine	350–965	1,650
Lounge suite	200–2,000	50,000
Double bed	100–800	4,000
Set of bed sheets	50 +	
Duvet/bed quilt	60 +	
Iron	40 +	
Dinner set (new)	30–40	
21″ TV set	450	
DVD player (basic)	400	

Power in NZ is 220 volt 50 cycle. Unless your appliances are dual voltage you will need to leave your appliances at home. If you are acquiring new appliances make sure they will accept both power systems. Many are made for both systems and all that you will need is an adapter. Whiteware normally refers to such items as fridges, freezers, washing machines and dryers.

OTHER COSTS

Public schooling (where charged for) will cost around NZ$150 per year, excluding uniforms, and kindergarten (full day) about NZ$135 per week. Private schools may charge NZ$10,000 per annum.

Average household expenses will vary between different families and areas but a household defined as 2.7 people can expect to have an expenditure of NZ$500–NZ$1,000 per week. This figure includes all food, housing (mortgage, rates), power, appliances, furniture, apparel, transport, personal items, newspapers, alcohol, health, savings and leisure services.

Healthcare

New Zealand has a very good standard of healthcare and a public health system that is available to everyone. Routine visits to the doctor and dentist have to be paid for (see page 219) but more costly services are usually free.

Free health services include:

- Public hospital treatment.
- 24-hour emergency treatment at hospitals and A&E clinics.
- Most laboratory tests and X-rays.
- Pregnancy and child-birth care (if you are referred to a midwife or specialist by your doctor).
- Plunket childcare see page 224.
- Basic dental care for school children.
- Breast screening for women aged 50–65.

Subsidised services include:

- Prescription items.
- Physiotherapists, chiropractors and osteopaths when

referred by a General Practitioner (GP).

CHOOSING A GP

To register with a GP you need to find one close to you and provide the receptionist with your address, phone number and family details. Also provide previous medical records if possible. There are no restrictions as to which GP you choose or where your GP is located. You can also change GP if you wish.

Most surgery hours are from 8am–6pm. Some may also open late one evening and Saturday mornings. In an emergency a GP will visit your home. The practice nurse usually handles routine checks like smears, blood pressure tests and immunisation.

If you require specialist medical care your GP will refer you to a specialist. If you have insurance you will be able to have private care. Waiting times will vary depending on the area and the type of service required.

HOSPITALS

There are 80 public hospitals in New Zealand and some provide facilities for the elderly or disabled.

The ambulance service is provided on a non-profit community-based system and you may be asked to make a payment of between NZ$45 and NZ$67.50 to help with running costs.

Contact details for all doctors, specialists, after hours and other medical centres, hospitals and midwives are found in the front of the telephone book.

The Plunket Society provides free care for mothers and their babies, which includes child health advice, parenting advice and development checks. Contact www.plunket.org.nz.

PRESCRIPTIONS

Prescriptions are dispensed by registered pharmacists and you can choose where you want to go. Standard costs are between NZ$3–NZ$15 per item and are free for children under six. Private health care provides immediate access to private hospitals and clinics for a range of services depending on the policy you choose. You are still entitled to free health services if you have insurance.

ACCIDENT INSURANCE

Accident insurance is a scheme managed by the Accident Compensation Corporation (ACC) and covers all personal injuries whether suffered at home, work or during sports or other leisure activities. This scheme means that you cannot sue anyone for compensation or damages if you are injured, suffer a medical mishap, sexual assault or abuse. Compensation may be paid for loss of income if you are unable to work. For further information contact www.acc.govt.nz.

SERVICES FOR PEOPLE AGED OVER 65

Services include home support, caregiver services and 24-hour residential care. The level of government subsidy depends on individual circumstances. For further information contact www.winz.govt.nz.

Useful websites

Health and Disability Commissioner which deals with
patient rights – www.hdc.org.nz.

HealthEd provides brochures on health matters –
www.healthed.govt.nz.

Ministry of Health provides information on the public
health system – www.moh.govt.nz.

Arthritis Foundation of New Zealand
– www.arthritis.org.nz.

Services for disabled people and their families –
www.ccs.org.nz.

Deaf Association – www.deaf.co.nz.

Diabetes New Zealand – www.diabetes.org.nz.

Eldernet provides information on retirement housing,
residential and hospital care of the elderly
– www.eldernet.co.nz.

Consumer health information – www.everybody.co.nz.

A–Z health guide and directory of health practitioners –
www.health.net.nz.

Directory of health professionals
– www.healthpages.co.nz.

Breast and cervical screening services
– www.healthywomen.org.nz.

Services for the intellectually impaired and their families –
www.ihc.org.nz.

Presbyterian support community services and counselling
– www.ps.org.nz.

Parents of visually impaired – www.pvi.org.nz.

The Royal New Zealand Foundation for the Blind –
www.rnzfb.org.nz.

Women's health services – www.womens-health.org.nz./
health.

DRIVING

Driving is relatively straightforward in New Zealand as traffic is light, the distance between towns is reasonably short and roads and signs are well maintained. There are few multi-lane highways. Unsealed back-roads in the country can be a hazard and care must be taken.

If you have a valid, unrestricted and current driver's licence from your home country, or an international driving permit you will be able to drive in New Zealand for 12 months before you require a New Zealand driver's licence.

Legal requirements

◆ New Zealanders drive on the left-hand side of the road.

◆ There are three phases to the traffic lights – red (stop), orange (get ready), and green (go).

◆ The speed limit is 100km/h (60mph) on the open roads and motorways. Central Auckland has a speed limit of

80km/h and built-up areas are usually 30–50km/h. (30mph).

♦ Do not drink and drive, as this is a very serious offence. The police can stop you and there are often random road stops or checks at any time of the day or night to breathalyse drivers. If you are stopped you will be required to blow into a plastic bag or speak into a machine that measures the amount of alcohol in your breath. If you refuse this test you will be taken to a testing centre where you will have another test and a sample of your blood will be taken.

♦ You will not be covered by your insurance if you have an accident while driving and are over the legal limit for alcohol. If you are convicted, you will automatically lose your licence, and be heavily fined or be put in jail.

♦ LSZ means the speed limit is restricted due to unsafe driving conditions like poor visibility, animals on the road, bad weather, pedestrians, school children or cyclists.

♦ Speed cameras and radar abound and plain clothes traffic officers and police are a speed deterrent.

♦ The law requires the driver to give way to any traffic approaching or crossing on the driver's *right* if you are at:
  – a 'Give Way' sign
  – a 'Stop' sign – stop completely then give way to all traffic – do not go over the line or you will be fined
  – going straight ahead – give way to all traffic coming straight through from your right

- turning – give way to all vehicles not turning
- turning left – give way to all vehicles coming towards you that are turning right
- turning right – give way to vehicles on your right that are turning right.

◆ Safety belts must be worn at all times in the front and back by all occupants of the car.

◆ You are responsible for ensuring that all children under five years must be in an approved restraint or safety seat.

◆ Safety helmets are compulsory and must be worn by all cyclists and motorcyclists. They must conform to the New Zealand Standard and be securely fastened and can be purchased at cycle shops. There is a fine of NZ$55 for breaking this law

Parking

◆ You are not allowed to park on or beside a yellow line or within six metres of an intersection or a pedestrian crossing.

◆ Parking signs with red writing on a white background apply at all times.

◆ It is illegal to park facing oncoming traffic. Parking must be the same way as the traffic flow.

◆ Parking signs with white writing on a blue background apply from Monday to Saturday, 8.00am–6.00pm.

The Automobile Association

Copies of *The Road Code* for both motorists and

motorcyclists will provide valuable information and is available from Automobile Association offices and bookshops. Membership of the AA is recommended for free, emergency roadside breakdown service and towage and free legal advice for accidents, parking and speeding tickets. Maps, various publications and discounts on services and accommodation are also available. If you are a member in another country you may be entitled to reciprocal benefits, but you will need your membership card. Contact the AA in NZ on free phone 0800 500 444 or email: www.nzaa.co.nz.

PURCHASING A VEHICLE

Vehicles or private cars are the most common way of getting around New Zealand. Unfortunately, because of the small population and high level of car ownership, it is uneconomic for many public transport companies to operate. There are 2.3 million plus vehicles and many families own two cars. Until 1970 most cars and motorbikes were of British or Australian origin. Today Japanese vehicles dominate the market and there are also Fords, Holdens, Mercedes, BMWs, Jaguars, Land Rovers and Harley Davidson, Ducati, BMW and Triumph motorbikes.

Purchasing a car is relatively simple and inexpensive in New Zealand as the deregulated market means Japanese imports are readily available. A second hand reliable family car can be purchased from NZ$1,000 up to NZ$50,0000. New cars range from NZ$20,000 to about NZ$80,000 depending on the make.

Car fairs

Car fairs in Auckland, Wellington and Christchurch are a good place to start and cost about NZ$12.50–NZ$15.00 to visit. Held most weekends, the seller waits with his car for a buyer. Car inspection services are available on site to help protect the buyer and it is a good opportunity to see what is available and to gauge prices. It still pays to research thoroughly before you buy.

Car auctions

Auctions are another way to purchase an inexpensive car ranging in price from NZ$1,200–NZ$5,000, but there is no opportunity to test drive so you need to be very knowledgeable or to have good advice.

Car registration

Any car you buy must have a Warrant of Fitness (WOF) and the annual registration must last for a reasonable period. The WOF certificate, which proves the car is roadworthy, must be valid for six months, but less than 28 days old when you purchase the car. To transfer registration you and the seller must fill out a form, which can be filed at any post office. The papers take ten days to be processed and arrive by mail. It is the seller's responsibility to transfer ownership and pay any costs involved.

Registration costs about NZ$200 for twelve months or it can be purchased for a six month period. It is also advisable to organise your insurance from the day you purchase, even if it is only third party insurance. This is cheap and will cover you if you damage another car.

Motoring costs

◆ Petrol: NZ$1.10 approximately per litre, unleaded and readily available in towns and cities. Make sure your tank is full before travelling on long stretches between some country towns. Diesel is also available as is LPG gas. Prices will fluctuate in town and country areas.

◆ Registration fee: NZ$160 per year (depends on size and type of car).

◆ Warrant of Fitness: NZ$30 for a car (required every 6-12 months depending on the age of the vehicle).

◆ Full insurance: NZ$630–NZ$7,500 per year based on the car value, the city area, and whether the driver is aged 30 or over.

It is also advisable to make sure the car is free of debt by making a credit check. Phone toll free NZ 0800 0800 658 934. You will need the licence plate and chassis numbers to confirm the ownership.

RENTAL VEHICLES

Rental cars, campervans and mobile homes all require a valid driving licence and you must be at least 21 years old. The insurance premiums will be less for those aged 26 years and over. Because minor rental car accidents are very common, insurance premiums are high. Some companies will waiver the insurance excess for a daily payment of NZ$10–20. Some areas of New Zealand, like the Ninety Mile beach and unsealed country roads are not covered by insurance. Read the small print and compare rates as charges vary between large well known companies such as:

Avis – www.avis.com

Hertz – www.hertz.co.nz
Budget – www.budget.co.nz
www.apexrentals.co.nz
www.nationalcar.com

and the smaller independent companies:

Pegasus (0800 803 580) – www.rentalcars.co.nz
Shoestring (0800 746 378) – www.carhire.co.nz/
shoestring

In Auckland, Wellington and Christchurch, ring about New Zealand Rental Cars NZ freephone 0800 455565 and ask for John Sommerville (excellent service and very reasonable). www.rentalcare.co.nz.

The easiest way to compare rates and offers is to phone around using *Yellow Pages*.

Always check kilometre rates, whether GST is included, minimum hire periods, bonds and insurance cover and carefully read the rental agreement before you sign. If you decide on the cheaper end of the market which is usually good value, do a thorough interior and exterior investigation of the upholstery, bodywork, tyres, damage to paint work, stone chips and lights with the company before you take the car. You will receive a form which you both sign to verify previous damage. It also pays to do a quick drive and check brakes and comfort before you leave as a lot of the cars are second hand and there is a big turnover. Prices tend to be higher in summer and more competitive in Auckland so it is advisable to plan ahead and book in advance.

Campervans are an ideal way to see the country and there are numerous camping sites around the country with basic facilities. Or you can find a remote spot beside a beach or near a hidden hotwater stream, far away from the madding throngs. Most will sleep 4–6 people, and have toilet, shower and kitchen facilities.

Rates start from approximately NZ$100 per day depending on the season. Contact:

Maui – www.maui.co.nz
Britz – www.britz.co.nz
www.nzmotorhomes.co.nz
Kea Campers – www.kea.co.nz
Backpacker Caravans –
www.backpackercampervans.com

MOTORBIKES
Motorbikes are also a fun way to explore New Zealand, but you will require a valid motorcycle licence. Contact NZ Motorcycle Rentals – www.nzbike.com.

COACHES, SHUTTLE AND BACKPACKER BUSES
Bus travel in New Zealand is inexpensive and well organised with the bonus of friendly and knowledgeable drivers. The main service to the bigger towns and tourist areas is operated by Intercity. Newmans (part of Intercity) covers most of the North Island (Northliner Express covers Northland), and from Christchurch to Milford via Mt Cook and Queenstown. Guthrey's Express also offer a competitive service on both islands. Contact

details:

    www.intercitycoach.co.nz

    www.newmanscoach.co.nz

    www.nzhere.com

    www.nzinfo.com/northliner

    www.sceniccoachtours.co.nz

    www.johnstons.co.nz

Shuttle buses are smaller, have more flexibility and often pick up and drop off at your accommodation and offer coverage of most of the tourist areas. Contact your local tourist information centre for details.

Backpacker buses cater specifically for this market and offer 'Hop-On-Hop-Off' passes which last from several days to weeks and cover many parts of the country. The main companies are Kiwi Experience and Magic Travellers Network, although check with the tourist information centre for alternatives. Contact details:

    enquiries@kiwiex.co.n

    info@magicbus.co.nz

    www.kiwiexperience.com

    www.magicbus.co.uk

    www.vanawaytours.co.nz

TRAINS

Auckland runs a regular commuter train service. Wellington has the best regular commuter train service. Renowned for the stunning scenery is the Tranz-Alpine journey from Christchurch to Greymouth via Arthurs Pass. The Tranz Coastal runs from Picton to Christchurch and the Northerner from Wellington to Auckland.

Contact:
    www.tranzscenic.co.nz
    www.foveauxexpress.co.nz

AIR TRAVEL

Air New Zealand and Quantas both provide a domestic and international service. Air New Zealand owns Eagle Air and Air Nelson to fly to the regions. Quantas focuses on the main trunk routes and links up with Nelson-based regional carrier Origin Pacific. Mount Cook Airlines, Freedom Air and commuter airlines connect the smaller towns. There are numerous small aircraft and helicopter companies, found mainly near tourist centres. Great Barrier Airlines will fly you to the outer islands in the Auckland Harbour. Popular rides are flights to the blasted crater of Mount Tarawera near Rotorua and the South Island's breathtaking flight from Mount Cook's airfield onto the Tasman Glacier. Soundsair fly the Cook Strait and Stewart Island Flights and Air Chathams will take you south. Contact details:
    www.airnewzealand.co.nz
    www.quantas.co.nz
    www.originpacific.co.nz
    www.freedom.co.nz

Airport Shuttle Buses:
    www.supershuttle.co.nz
    www.airbus.co.nz

SEA TRAVEL

Water transport ranges from high-thrill jet boats that race over river rapids to stately steamers, ferries, launches and large yachts, even an America's Cup yacht is available for excursions or charter. Fullers in the Bay of Islands offers ferry rides and water taxis to the many islands and Fullers in the Auckland Harbour has regular commuter ferry services to Devonport, Birkenhead, Gulf Harbour and islands like Waiheke and the bird sanctuary Tiri Tiri Matenga. Ferry operators take vehicles from the North to the South Islands across Cook Strait between Wellington and Picton in the Marlborough Sounds. The Interisland line operates The Lynx catamaran and The Interislander ferry which takes from 90 minutes to three-and-a-half hours depending on the weather conditions and the boat's speed. There is also a launch service across Foveaux Strait to Stewart Island. Contact details:

www.interislandline.co.nz

www.foveauxexpress.co.nz

Before You Leave

GENERAL CHECKLIST

- **Banks and credit cards**. Your present bank should be able to help set up an account in New Zealand so that you can use your credit card and make withdrawals when you arrive.

- **Pensions**. Check your entitlement to the government pension fund of your country. Get up-to-date benefit statements of all your pensions, both private and work related so you are clear about your situation.

- **Investments**. Obtain up-to-date statements and valuations of all investments along with supporting ownership documentation and contact details.

- **Life insurance**. Review all policies and decide whether to cancel, put on hold or cash up, bearing in mind that you may require cover until you reach New Zealand. Also remember if you have an illness or condition covered on your current policy it may be more expensive to start again in another country. Life insurance and income protection plans in New Zealand will ensure that you are covered financially against any eventuality. Contact your bank or financial advisor.

◆ Also check insurance cover for your goods in transit.

◆ **Medical insurance** is still necessary as there are limits to what the ACC can pay and the claimant may have to pay part of the costs. Check as some costs may also be recoverable. (See page 234 for more details.) Some people prefer to have full medical insurance to cover illnesses and provide immediate medical attention if required. Again this can be considered once you have arrived in New Zealand.

◆ **Wills** are essential, as is an enduring Power of Attorney to ensure your assets are dealt with in accordance with your wishes after death or incapacitation. A solicitor is usually best for this.

◆ Remember to take the following original documents:
  – birth certificates
  – marriage certificates
  – academic qualifications
  – references from previous employers
  – curriculum vitae
  – credit references
  – an international driver's licence or permit
  – Automobile Association membership for reciprocal benefits.

◆ Ownership of assets is best discussed with a solicitor, because New Zealand's matrimonial laws may differ from your previous home country.

◆ **Tax** (see Chapter 10). It is recommended that you speak to a New Zealand accountant before you leave your home country as the tax regime is very different in New Zealand, and you may be able to reduce your tax liability.

◆ **Money**. You will need to make a budget of your finances especially for arrival, when you will need funds for rent or hotels, car rental and living expenses until you start working. Plan to have New Zealand money in $5, $10 and $20 notes. Anything bigger may be regarded as unusual.

◆ **Clothing**. As the weather is changeable and you are travelling from one season to another, take and wear layers that can be taken off or put on if required. A light raincoat is useful.

◆ Children's toys for the trip and arrival.

◆ **Exchange rates** – shop around as the difference on a large amount of money from, for example, the sale of your house can be thousands of dollars and better in your pocket than anyone else's. When you are in New Zealand you can review your retirement and savings goals and the options available to you in New Zealand. Contact details:
  www.broadbase.co.nz
  www.amp.nz
  www.miplc.co.uk
  londonmbs@cba.com.au
  www.moneycorp.com
  www.hifx.co.uk

DEPARTURE CHECK LIST

◆ Check that all of your financial, taxation and legal matters are sorted out early and finalised before you leave.

◆ Make sure all your travel plans are complete.

◆ Give your new contact details to your family and friends before you leave.

◆ Ensure you have all your original documents like birth certificates, university or similar degrees and awards, trade qualifications, family medical records, references and children's school reports. Make copies of all of your documents to keep in a safe place.

◆ Encourage your children to make a photo album of family and friends to provide a history of life in your old country. Include email, phone numbers and contact addresses.

◆ Become familiar with New Zealand's road code before you arrive.

◆ If you require a post box until you have a permanent address, contact New Zealand Post or one of the private companies offering a similar service.

◆ It would also be advisable to contact employment agencies in your home country for a job on arrival. See Chapter 7 for contact details and web addresses.

THE MOVE

International moving is very different from the ordinary domestic move. Specialist companies whose main business is overseas removal are often able to offer competitive rates as they ship frequent consignments to other countries. These companies generally have depots throughout the UK and will be able to visit you at home to provide a free estimate of the costs involved. Some companies will complete a comprehensive pre-move survey and then design a personally tailored moving plan to suit your budget.

Things that you may require urgently like business computers and baby equipment can be sent by air. All companies will provide experienced packers, containers and use export quality heavy-duty materials for wrapping. For vulnerable goods they will supply strong timber cases.

They will also advise on the best route and method of moving your belongings overseas.

◆ Ensure the firm you choose is a member of the Overseas Group of the British Association of Removers (BAR), or the International Movers Federation (FIDI).

◆ Make sure the company has suitable insurance such as the International Movers Mutual Insurance (IMMI). It is important to ensure that insurance cover commences once payment has been made, so that you are covered and there are no extra costs when you receive the shipment in your new country.

◆ If time and speed are important, goods can be sent by airfreight, which will be expensive. Costs can be reduced if the company you choose offers a groupage container service, where the space is shared by other shipments going to the same destination.

◆ Check that you have marine insurance cover in the event of an unforeseen accident in transit or other problems such as delays.

◆ To save you time, money and unnecessary red tape ask your moving company to arrange customs clearance, and transit bonds (required to ensure transit through foreign ports).

◆ Some companies will arrange for a destination agent to take care of your belongings and complete all the paperwork for delivery to your new address.

◆ If required, some companies will unpack your possessions at your new home.

◆ It may be useful to find a company with storage space in your home country in case there is a delay in your planned move.

◆ Check whether they will ship your car and deal with all the paperwork and customs clearances.

◆ Do they offer an after-shipment service where they will pack and send you something that you can't obtain in your new country?

Start thinking and planning the move at least three to six months before your departure by contacting different companies for information packs. Approach two or three firms for an estimate and remember it may take two to

three weeks for the appointment date. It is important that
you have an initial idea of the items you want shipped,
although the estimator will guide you. Contact details:

www.alliedpickfords.co.uk **UK** freephone 0800 289
229

Britannia – www.britannia-movers.co.uk

Bishop's Blatchpack UK freephone 0800 616 425

www.copsey.com or UK freephone 0800 289 658

www.pss.uk.com

www.anglopacific.co.uk

www.johnmason.com or email sales@johnmason.com

sales@p-s-s.co.uk

DECIDING WHAT TO TAKE

This is a major decision as it is expensive to ship goods
that will prove unnecessary in your new country.
Remember that you pay for volume when shipping goods.

This can be a very stressful time so it is important to have
some familiar items to help your family settle. Ask friends
in New Zealand for suggestions and remember that quality
furniture and some household items will be more expensive
to purchase in your new country. You may decide to take
household goods like furniture, linen, crockery, cutlery and
furnishings (rugs and curtains), your car (see page 246) and
your children's favourite toys. A carton of toys will cost a
small amount (approx. £30) to take and provide excitement
when it arrives. Limit each child to x amount of boxes so
that they can choose what they want to take.

The moving company Allied Pickfords sell a children's
storybook called *Moving Overseas* which will help small

children to understand what is happening. Bikes and sporting equipment are relatively inexpensive to ship, but make sure they are very clean.

As your shipment will take from 6–14 weeks to arrive it may be advisable to take some toys for arrival either on the plane or as unaccompanied luggage. Some airlines are amenable to *extra baggage allowance for first time migrants.*

Electrical and electronic equipment

The electrical power system in New Zealand supplies alternating current at 240 volts 50 hertz. Electrical equipment from a 110-volt system needs transformers.

Stereos, computers and Play Stations should work in New Zealand. Although the television will not receive broadcasts, the monitor may be useful for VHS videos or Play Station.

If you want to bring items like a CD player, hairdryer or television make sure that the items are compatible with New Zealand's electrical system.

Remember that it may not be worth bringing electrical appliances or electronic goods with you as you may not be able to get them serviced in New Zealand. Some specialised equipment may not work properly, even with a transformer, if it is designed for a different frequency.

Phones, faxes and other telecommunications equipment of all sorts that you use in your home country should be left behind as they may not work with the local network or be properly repaired if necessary.

One of the biggest problems with any of the above is the extremes of temperature shipments encounter on the long voyage to New Zealand. New Zealand is a high-tech industrialised western nation and the latest electronic and electrical appliances are readily and inexpensively available.

FINANCIAL ARRANGEMENTS IN NEW ZEALAND

For speedy setting up of new accounts in New Zealand, it is useful to bring credit references from your bank, gas, power and telephone companies. Particularly useful is evidence of your mortgage repayments and of your home ownership or regular rental payments, previous insurance policies, pay slips and references, and any credit checks that may have been done. The more information you can provide the easier it is for the lender to be confident of your financial history.

18
What You Can and Can't
Bring into New Zealand

When you are immigrating to New Zealand and arriving for the first time with your belongings, there is no tax or duty to be paid on them *as long as they are for your personal use only* and not for sale or exchange to other people. This includes your clothing and most other personal belongings such as jewellery, which may be new but must be for your own personal use.

Household goods like stereos, furniture, refrigerators and homewares must have been owned and used by you before you arrive in New Zealand in order to qualify for duty free entry. Check the price of whiteware in New Zealand before you leave, as it may be easier and cheaper to purchase new with a guarantee.

The New Zealand Customs Service pamphlet *Advice on Importing Goods into New Zealand* provides full information about importing goods. Their email address is feedback@customs.govt.nz.

MOTOR VEHICLES AND BOATS

An important decision is whether to take your car or start anew. You may not be able to obtain spare parts in New Zealand and have it serviced satisfactorily.

There are no restrictions on importing your own car or boat into New Zealand but you will need to ensure that it meets all design and safety regulations before it can be registered. Also there are only some categories of left-hand-drive vehicles that can be used on New Zealand roads. Contact the Land Transport Safety Authority www.itsa.govt.nz for their most relevant fact sheet and then find out if it is suitable to export from the contact details below or your shipping company.

If your car or boat has been owned and used by you for at least one year before the date of shipping there is no duty to be paid. After arrival, as long as your vehicle or boat is kept and used by you for at least two years, there won't be any customs charges to be paid.

Shipping costs

Shipping and insurance costs are payable usually before you leave. In New Zealand customs duty (see above) may be payable on the UK purchase price, duty and shipping costs. Also payable are other costs which include unpacking the container, customs charges, port clearance, quarantine inspection, Warrant of Fitness and registration. Contact www.customs-govt.nz

Contact reputable freight companies for written quotes. They will arrange the export once you have approval to emigrate.

Shipping your vehicle

A car is safest shipped in a sealed 20-foot container, and usually any contents you want to pack inside travel free of charge. Most companies will provide mats, seat covers and bags of silica desiccant as protection against condensation damage. Motorbikes are normally shipped in wooden crates and personal items can be packed inside.

Costs payable before you leave include moving your vehicle from your home to the warehouse (where it will be packed in a container) and shipping and marine insurance cover (normally between 1–2% of the vehicle's value).

Upon arrival in New Zealand your vehicle, motorbikes or bikes will be inspected. If found to be contaminated, they be steam-cleaned and you will need to pay this cost. Transit takes 3–4 weeks from the UK. Local customs brokers can assist you and your shipping company may have suitable contacts to simplify the procedure.

For more information contact the Land Transport Authority for all aspects of transport regulation at www.ltsa.govt.nz.

Other useful contacts are:
    www.doreebonner.co.uk
    www.karmanshipping.com
    www.robinsons-intl.com
    email: moving@dbonner.co.uk
    interconti@btconnect.com

PETS

Nearly all kinds of animals are prohibited from being brought into New Zealand except for cats and dogs, which are allowed in from most countries. However, they will need to meet certain requirements prior to leaving their homeland and may have to enter quarantine when they arrive. The only exception is Australia as pets can easily be moved between both countries. Cats and dogs from the United Kingdom and Hawaii don't need to be quarantined but do require a series of tests. Animals from other countries may require up to a 30-day quarantine stay, which could cost approximately NZ$1,000. Again, it is best to start planning well ahead, as you will need to check this information well in advance.

Moving your pets is fairly straightforward, using special pet moving services. More than a million of our furry four-legged friends safely fly worldwide each year. It is important to allow plenty of time (more than six months) for reservations to be made and all documentation to be completed. A reputable company will have a vet in attendance, provide boarding and grooming if required, use IATA-approved travel kennels and offer collection of your animal. Ask at least three different companies for advice and costs and quotes. Contact the Import Management Office of the Ministry of Agriculture and Forestry if you need further information – www.maf.govt.nz. For further information contact the official website: www.defra.gov.uk.

Other useful contacts:
www.parair.co.uk or parair@btinternet.com

www.ladyhaye.co.uk or email info@ladyhaye.co.uk
www.airpets.com or email Airpets@compuserve.com
 Animal Airlines: Tel (UK) 0870 833 8020, Fax: 0870
 833 8022, 833 8021
 Golden Arrow Shippers: Tel (UK) 01588 680 240, Fax:
 01 588 680 414

FIREARMS

Guns and other weapons can only be used in New
Zealand for lawful purposes and a firearms licence is
required. It is illegal to have a gun for self-defence. There
are strict controls on the importation of firearms or guns.
You will require a firearms licence and permit from the
New Zealand Police. The recommended way to do this is
to leave your firearms behind and then obtain the licence
and permit to import from the New Zealand Police once
you have arrived.

DRUGS

Drugs must not be brought into New Zealand. You will
be arrested if caught doing so. If you need to use
medicines that include narcotics you will require a letter
from your doctor stating the reason for their use.

Arriving in New Zealand

CUSTOMS DECLARATIONS

New Zealand is free of many of the world's serious pests. Anyone can unknowingly introduce these serious threats to New Zealand's agriculture and environment. As you enter the country you are required by law to declare all plant and animal matter that you have brought with you. You must complete an Agriculture and Customs Declaration on arrival. You must declare the following if you have them with you:

- Food of any sort and the products and ingredients used for preparing food.
- Plants and parts of plants, either alive or dead, including cane, straw or rattan.
- Equipment used with animals, or animals alive or dead.
- Camping gear, golf clubs, hiking boots, shoes, equestrian equipment and used bicycles.
- Biological specimens.

Some items can only be brought into New Zealand if you have previously obtained written permission. These include reptiles, fruit, meat, honey and bird nests.

> **It is extremely important that you declare any items that are restricted.**

If you are in any doubt about any items, declare them. If you declare restricted items you will not be charged with any offence. However, if you try to bring in restricted items and do not declare them, you will be prosecuted and liable to face heavy fines or other sentences. New Zealand is very serious about protecting its agricultural economy and environment. If you have goods to declare you will need to go through the 'red channel' at the airport, where a Ministry of Agriculture and Forestry (MAF) Quarantine Service Officer will inspect them.

If you have items which cannot be brought into New Zealand, and you have declared them as requested, the goods will simply be taken away from you and you are free to go. Some items may be fumigated and returned to you. Contact website www.maf.govt.nz/biosecurity/imports.

ARRIVAL CHECKLIST

Things to do as soon as possible after arrival in your new country.

♦ Apply for an Inland Revenue Number (see page 150).
♦ Safe custody boxes are available at your bank for a small fee for storage of jewellery and important documents until you settle.

20 Living and Leisure in New Zealand

THE WEATHER

Lying between 37 and 47 degrees south of the Tropic of Capricorn the two islands of New Zealand have a moderate, maritime climate. This means that the weather can change with great rapidity because the smaller landmass is surrounded by water and situated in the Roaring Forties. The prevailing winds blow from east to west and range from gentle breezes, which are welcome in summer's humidity, to winter's cold southerly from the Antarctic. The capital tends to be referred to as 'Windy Wellington' by those living outside the area. Between cities a competitive spirit is found not only in sports but in the weather as well.

The warmest months are December, January, February and March with temperatures ranging between 20 and 33 degrees Celsius. June, July and August are winter's coldest months with temperatures from 5–15 degrees Celsius. The South Island is generally cooler than the North with snow appearing mainly on the mountains and surrounding areas of both islands.

◆ The North Island's rainfall is fairly evenly distributed and averages 1300mm per year. However the western side of the South Island has a rainfall of over 7500mm while the eastern side is protected by the Southern Alps mountain range and has an annual rainfall of only about 330mm.

◆ Because New Zealand is prone to earthquakes, which are very small and of little concern, it is advisable to take a few simple precautions. Information on what to do and how to prepare for an earthquake and other emergencies is inside the front or back cover of *Yellow Pages* or visit www.civildefence.govt.nz.

GENERAL INFORMATION

◆ Workplaces must have smoke free areas and smoking is totally banned in the work environment. Restaurants usually have smoking and non-smoking sections. The sale of cigarettes to anyone under the age of 18 is prohibited.

◆ Citizen's Advice Bureau (CAB) is a confidential and free local service available to anyone, whether they are a visitor to New Zealand or a citizen who requires a contact or help in any way about any of the following:
  – free legal services
  – employment rights
  – housing and tenancy issues
  – free budgeting advice
  – health and welfare issues
  – consumer rights

– interpreting and translation services
– education and training
– personal and family issues
– unemployment problems.
Contact NZ free phone: 0800 367 222 for your closest contact or visit www.cab.org.nz.

- **Fireworks** can only be purchased the week before Guy Fawkes and most families attend community displays.

- **Women** have the same status as men in New Zealand and it is illegal to discriminate against anyone on the basis of sex. Women do not lose their status if married. Women hold the five highest positions in the country, which includes the Governor General and Prime Minister.

- **Police** in New Zealand have a wide range of duties which include enforcing the law, traffic patrols, carrying out investigations, search and rescue and The Youth Education Service. They normally do not carry guns and it is illegal for anyone to carry or own guns or other such weapons. *New Zealand Police have high standards of moral and ethical behaviour and are well respected in the community.* They are very approachable and will quickly respond if you feel threatened or intimidated by anyone.

- **Violence** towards or assaulting another person in New Zealand is illegal whether it is a kick, punch or unwanted sexual attention. This includes family (and adopted) members, the elderly or children. Teachers are not allowed to hit children.

- **Telecommunications** and Internet services are very competitive in New Zealand and the biggest providers are Telecom New Zealand and Telstra-Saturn. Although the market is deregulated and there are other providers, Telecom operates most of the 'free local call' networks. There are about 20 different companies and it pays to compare prices, especially for international or long distance calls. There are both analogue and digital communications networks, which cover most of the country. Most New Zealand homes have a telephone and a colour television and more than half of the population has a computer, with over a quarter having an Internet connection. In 2000, Telecom New Zealand's CEO Theresa Gattung said 'that according to independent research, New Zealand's Internet subscriber base would grow by more than 20% per year and hit 1.5 million by 2004'. Today, New Zealanders are the biggest users in the world.

- **Television** is available free-to-air on five national channels. There are also regional television stations and other private channels. Pay Sky or satellite television has movies, sports, documentaries, CNN, or BBC news magazine programmes and teenage drama channels. There are also other local television channels that have to be paid for.

- **Radio** is very competitive with 120 privately-owned stations, several Maori language stations and two-state owned stations. These are the National Radio with current affairs programmes and Concert Fm which specialises in classical music.

- **Religion** in New Zealand is predominantly Christian in one of its many forms, which includes Catholic, Anglican, Baptist, Methodist, and Presbyterian faiths. There are many different ethnic religions also with their own places of worship. Generally there is tolerance and respect amongst different groups regarding an individual's chosen faith.

- **Shopping and food** in New Zealand is available most days of the year. Supermarkets are usually open before 9am and close late at 8 or 9pm. Fresh meat and delicatessen serveries are available in most of the supermarkets. Some takeaway food bars and petrol stations are open 24 hours, seven days a week. Every type of food is now available and there are many speciality shops such as organic and Chinese. There is a thriving café society. Cafés, bars and restaurants abound throughout New Zealand, especially Wellington, which has more bars and cafés per capita than New York. Most restaurants are licensed to serve alcohol, and cafés are often less expensive with Bring Your Own (BYO) which means bring your own wine. Alcohol is usually available to purchase seven days a week.

- **Meeting people** is fairly straightforward. In a business or formal environment, it is usual to shake their right hand with your right and look them in the eye as you repeat their surname or family name preceded by a Mr or Ms (which is preferred by most women). However, as it is an informal society most people use first names. It is okay to ask a woman how they would prefer to be addressed.

- **Dinner parties and social events**. If you are invited to someone's home it is customary to take a bottle of wine and for dinner parties to ask, 'What can I bring?'. Often the hosts may decline your offer or sometimes suggest that you bring a salad or pre-dinner snacks, a dessert or after-dinner mints. Sometimes guests are asked to 'bring a plate' which actually means to bring a plate with some food on! Find out what sort of food is preferred.

- **Parties** are often referred to as a 'Do'. If it is a work 'do' management usually supply the drinks and snacks on a Friday after work. If it is organised by a friend or a club, everyone contributes with a plate and a bottle of something to drink or they chip in to help pay for it. It is all fairly informal and no one minds if you have to ask about anything that you are not sure of.

- **Weddings** can vary from very formal to a simple beach ceremony. Hats are optional but recommended in the summer sun.

- **Funerals** also vary and can be personalised according to the wishes of the family. Semi-formal dress is increasingly common although it is a mark of respect to wear a dark colour. An important exception is the tangi, the traditional Maori funeral. There are solemn rituals at which marae protocol is strictly observed.

- New Zealand celebrates **11 public holidays** per year and every person is entitled to them. If the day falls on a weekend there is a legal entitlement to the next day off work.

◆ **Daylight saving** applies on the first Sunday in October when all clocks are put forward. They are put back on the third Sunday in March.

◆ **Rubbish collection** and recycling is taken very seriously in New Zealand and will vary depending on where you live. Councils usually provide a bag which is left on the kerbside once a week. The North Shore, Auckland requires a sticker of NZ$1.00 on each bag put out but also provides recycling bins so that paper, plastics, tins and glass are sorted in the home. Inorganic collections are notified in advance as most councils do not regularly collect large items. Garden rubbish has to go to the local refuse centre and you can hire skips or large bins to fill over a weekend. Keen gardeners have a regular green collection that they pay for.

◆ Most New Zealanders do not have **servants or cooks** but may hire home help weekly for cleaning. Handymen or odd job contractors are often used to mow lawns or maintain gardens, do minor repairs or painting. Electrical, gas fitting and plumbing must be done by a registered tradesman. If you decide to employ anyone on this basis you need to ascertain costs first. Ask for a quote, that is a fixed price for the job, which once accepted must be done to that price unless you agree to a change. You can also ask for an estimate which is just that – an estimation of how much the job could cost. Find out how much more the final price will be before the job starts. Make sure everything is in writing. If you are unsure, contact your local CAB.

- **Marriages** are legal over 16 years of age. If either partner is under 20 parental consent may be required.

- **Divorce** can be simple as a couple only have to live apart for two years and it is granted automatically. New Zealand's divorce laws may differ from your country, so be aware. All matrimonial property is generally divided equally after three years of marriage whether it is a same sex or de facto relationship. Contact the Registrar of Births, Deaths and Marriages on www.dia.govt.nz.

- **Alcohol and the law**. Anyone over the age of 18 years can go into licensed premises and buy alcohol to drink. They may have to provide legal identification like a New Zealand Driver's Licence or a passport.

- Parents can supply those aged under 18 years of age with alcohol at a private social function or in their home.

- It is illegal to drink and drive.

CULTURE AND THE ARTS

New Zealand is proud her own culture embraces a strong tradition of Maori art and craft, Polynesian, European ancestry and other traditions. Maori have a wide range of performing arts – Kapa Haka, which includes haka, waiata and poi dancing. The national competitions are well supported by the general public. The Chinese community celebrate their New Year with traditional festivities. Many of the different ethnic groups will advertise their celebrations which give parts of New

Zealand, especially Auckland a colourful diversity.

Theatres, orchestras, opera and dance

Most cities have theatres, orchestras and sometimes opera companies of their own. Auckland is home to several modern dance companies while Wellington is the 'theatre capital' with three, full-time professional theatres. Wellington is also the home of the huge biannual International Festival of the Arts while Christchurch, New Plymouth, Tauranga and Nelson all host Arts Festivals.

Museums

Te Papa, The Museum of New Zealand, based on Wellington's waterfront showcases New Zealand art and culture often hosting international exhibitions. As does Auckland's Art Gallery, with crowd pleasing exhibitions like Monet, that broke all attendance records.

The film industry

The film industry has international status with the recent *The Lord of the Rings* trilogy winning Oscars. The cult series *Hercules* and *Xena* were filmed in Auckland and the more recent international teenage hit *The Tribe* was shot in Wellington.

SPORTS

Recreation and sport is where New Zealand comes into her own. New Zealanders enjoy playing sport and these rugged islands surrounded by water offer unlimited possibilities. There is hiking (tramping), skiing and cycling if you want to explore the outdoors; rugby, cricket, softball, basketball or netball if you enjoy team sports; and clubs where you can play tennis, swim, or participate in athletics.

New Zealanders love to be fit and there are many gymnasiums if you want a personal fitness programme.

The most popular sport is fishing and barbeques on a summer's evening will often have freshly caught fish (schnapper) on the menu. Because New Zealand has the best trout fishing in the world 23% of the population regularly fishes. There are no private waters and the licence fee is modest. The regulations are strictly observed and trout fishermen are noted for their sporting ethic.

There is no licence for sea fishing, but strict regulations and fines apply to fishing methods, maximum catches, fishing seasons and prohibited areas. Specific laws also apply to gathering shellfish. It is forbidden to sell or trade your catch. Breaking the fishing regulations including those governing the collection of wild shellfish is totally unacceptable and can result in heavy fines or imprisonment.

For more information about fresh water fishing contact the local office of Fish and Game NZ or visit www.fishandgame.org.nz. For information on sea fishing laws, contact the Ministry of Fisheries on www.fish.govt.nz.

For golfers there are plenty of clubs of an international standard and public courses that are not overcrowded and have reasonable fees.

Many New Zealanders own their own boats with the highest ownership per capita in the world. Children start with a 'P' class and learn to sail at clubs all over New Zealand, while adults cruise in everything from a sailer-trailer to ocean-going luxury craft.

For the more adventurous there is para-ponting, hang-gliding, sky-diving, white water rafting and bungee jumping. Extreme sports events are held in the South Island where contestants race from one coast to the other across the Southern Alps and, if that sounds a tad overdoing it, you can always run in the annual 'Round the Bays' along the Auckland waterfront.

21

Suggestions for Discovering New Zealand

WHERE TO GO

Decide if you want to fly between stops or travel by car, campervan or public transport (see Chapter 16). If using the latter, a New Zealand Travel Pass will offer a convenient and reasonably inexpensive way to explore the country with unlimited travel on the extensive rail and coach network, ferry and usually one flight. For more information contact www.bestpass.co.nz.

If flying, there are discounts available, especially if one travels at unpopular hours such as 7am or 10pm. Depending on the times spent at each location and the mode of travel, New Zealand can be comfortably explored in a month or two weeks allowing a week in each island. (See Chapter 12 for more details about each area.)

NORTH ISLAND HIGHLIGHTS

Auckland is the best place to start by heading on State Highway 1 up to Orewa and the Hibiscus Coast and on to

The Bay of Islands in Northland. Take a boat cruise around Paihia and Russell and visit historic Waitangi where the Treaty was signed and then head to the far north and Cape Reinga. Return via the Waipoua Kauri Forest on the West Coast and visit the Matakohe Kauri Museum en route to Auckland. You could stop for a swim at Helensville's Parakai Aquatic Park (hot pools) if you follow Highway 16.

Back in Auckland, take the ferry to Devonport, or cruise to Rangitoto or Waiheke Islands for the day and enjoy fine food and wine tasting. Also don't forget to visit the Auckland War Memorial Museum for a taste of history. Then head to Rotorua and experience the award-winning Tamaki Village hangi and concert, the geysers, boiling mud and a soak in the relaxing Polynesian Pools. A detour to Waitomo caves will take your breath away with magical underground limestone scapes, rivers and glow-worms. Then it's on to Taupo for great fishing and golf at the Wairaki Hotel.

Continue south through the spectacular Tongariro National Park and the volcanic landscape, where you can walk or hike the seven-hour Tongariro Crossing which skirts crater lakes and has astonishing views if you have time.

A week or ten days after you started your trip you will arrive in Wellington where a visit to Te Papa, the National Museum of NZ is a must, as is dining in the super cafés. If you travel back to Auckland go via the East Coast to Art Deco Napier and indulge yourself at the vineyards in the

Wairapa and Hawkes Bay on the way.

SOUTH ISLAND HIGHLIGHTS

Catch the ferry to Marlborough where kayaking and bird spotting are musts if there's time. Otherwise it's cycling around more than 50 superb wineries and on to Kaikoura for a meal of fresh crayfish, whale watching, and swimming with dolphins, seals and sharks. (Sperm whales in September to October and orcas, December to March.) Then Christchurch beckons with the charming French town of Akaroa and the TranzAlpine rail journey across to the west coast for the Fox and Franz Josef Glaciers. You can walk on them or do a heli-hike to really appreciate the splendour. If there is time, call into Aoraki, Mount Cook, the highest mountain in New Zealand for more mighty glaciers and good walks.

If you are driving, take your time down the west coast to the wild Fiordland area, where the calm waters of the 22km long Milford Sounds reflect the sheer peaks and on through to Doubtful Sounds where you need to stop for a cruise in this majestic country. Watch out for the biggest sandflies you will ever see!

Next is Queenstown for skiing, wonderful food, and bungee jumping and a few days are needed to explore the picturesque and historic Arrowtown and Cromwell. Then on to Otago for the wildlife and, of course, Bluff for the oysters if there is time.

ACCOMMODATION

New Zealand has many bed and breakfast places to stay that are very comfortable and good value. It is recommended that the *New Zealand B&B Directory* is purchased from any bookstore so bookings can be made ahead.

Accommodation websites

Golden Chain Motels – www.goldenchain.co.nz.
Mainstay Hotels – www.mainstay.co.nz.
AA Host Motel Accommodation
   – www.aatour-newzealand.co.nz.
AA New Zealand Accommodation Guide
   – www.aaguides.co.nz.
Scenic Circle Hotels and Resorts
   – www.scenic-circle.co.nz.
Jasons New Zealand Travel Channel – www.jasons.co.nz.
Contacts for Visitor Informatiom Centres
   – www.visitorinfo.co.nz.

Transport websites

Plan your route across and around Auckland using ferries, buses or/and trains – www.rideline.co.nz.
Timetables and fares of bus services within Hamilton City and the Waikato region – www.ew.govt.nz.
There is access to Wellington's bus and train timetables and fares at www.wrc.govt.nz./rt/pickroute.cfm.
Bus timetables for Christchurch – www.metroinfo.org.nz.
Dunedin bus timetables and fares – www.orcgovt.nz.

General information websites

These sites provide a national directory of Visitor

Information Centres on a strictly regional basis: www.visitinfo.co.nz and www.arrival.co.nz.

The Department of Conservation is responsible for maintaining the walking tracks and huts in the National Parks. Contact: www.doc.govt.nz/explore.

There is a general tourism website that lists National Parks under 'Top Resources' in the left hand menu bar: www.newzealandnz.co.nz.

Tourism New Zealand's promotional website includes many of the country's famous natural attractions and activities – www.purenz.com.

Useful Web Contacts

NEW ZEALAND BUSINESS DIRECTORIES

A'Courts are the most comprehensive and up-to-date database of products available in New Zealand – www.acourt.co.nz.

Pipers New Zealand Pages have thousands of websites providing a lot of information about New Zealand – www.piperpat.co.nz/nz.

NZ.com is dedicated to providing internet resources about New Zealand and for businesses and direct sales – www.nz.com/mainpage.html.

The New Zealand Chamber of Commerce site provides access to the Auckland, Wellington, Canterbury and Otago branches – www.chamber.co.nz.

UBD – New Zealand Business Directory contains details of over 152,990 businesses throughout the country – www.ubd.co.nz.

Kompass New Zealand is a business to business database which identifies contacts by product, service or industry – www.kompass.co.nz.

NEW ZEALAND SEARCH ENGINES

Access New Zealand provides a directory of websites maintained by NZ companies and organisations – www.accessnz.co.nz.

Telecom New Zealand Yellow Pages is a national directory of business contacts – www.yellowpages.-co.nz.

NZPages is a search engine and directory for New Zealand websites – www.nzpages.co.nz.

NEW ZEALAND GOVERNMENT

New Zealand Government Online is the official website which provides access to government services information and an overview of New Zealand – www.govt.nz.

The Ministry of Agriculture and Fisheries (MAF) works in conjunction with the Ministry of Foreign Affairs and Trade to win access for New Zealand products overseas. It certifies export products and protects New Zealand farms and wildlife from imported pests and diseases – www.maf.govt.nz.

The Ministry of Economic Development is the government's primary advisor on issues related to economics, industry and regional development. It also advises on overall business performance and the operation of markets – www.med.govt.nz.

Industry New Zealand helps to create a strong, vibrant and progressive economy by supporting New Zealand regions, industries and businesses – www.industrynz.govt.nz.

TRADE

Trade New Zealand facilitates leadership, trade and

international investments – www.tradenz.govt.nz.

New Zealand Customs Service manages risks from the movement of people, goods, and craft across the border, services in relation to border-meeting requirements of other agencies and strategic policy advice regarding border and revenue risks –
www.customs.govt.nz.

New Zealand Exporters Online have information on the wide range of quality products exported internationally – www.marketnewzealand.com.

New Zealand Trade Centre is a directory of New Zealand export companies – www.newzealandtradecentre.com.

INVESTMENT IN NEW ZEALAND

Investment in New Zealand details investment opportunities in New Zealand –
www.investmentnewzealand.govt.nz.

Industry New Zealand provides specialist advice and support to businesses or individual wanting to make major investments or establish new ventures in New Zealand – www.industrynzgovt.nz/invest-in-nz.

Index